LESSONS IN JAMAICA

Short-Term Missions in the Children's Homes of Jamaica

HEIDI HAAGENSON

outskirts press

Lessons Learned in Jamaica
Short-Term Missions in the Children's Homes of Jamaica
All Rights Reserved.
Copyright © 2022 Heidi Haagenson
v3.0

The opinions expressed in this manuscript are solely the opinions of the author and do not represent the opinions or thoughts of the publisher. The author has represented and warranted full ownership and/or legal right to publish all the materials in this book.

This book may not be reproduced, transmitted, or stored in whole or in part by any means, including graphic, electronic, or mechanical without the express written consent of the publisher except in the case of brief quotations embodied in critical articles and reviews.

Outskirts Press, Inc.
http://www.outskirtspress.com

ISBN: 978-1-9772-4888-6

Cover Design © 2022 www.gettyimages.com. All rights reserved - used with permission.
Cover Photo (c) 2022 Marti Carlson. All rights reserved - used with permission.

Outskirts Press and the "OP" logo are trademarks belonging to Outskirts Press, Inc.

PRINTED IN THE UNITED STATES OF AMERICA

"On the streets of Jamaica, I saw a small black boy, lonely, dirty, and hungry, with little hope of a good meal or a peaceful night's sleep. I became angry and said to God, 'Why did you permit this? Why don't you do something about it?' For a while God said nothing. Then he replied, 'I certainly did do something about it—I made you.'"

—Author Unknown

Chapter 1

INTRODUCTION

I BEGAN TRAVELING to Jamaica in 1995 when my church in Minnesota offered an opportunity to experience a short-term mission to Sunbeam Children's Home in St. Catherine, Jamaica. This mission would involve living and working in this children's home with thirty-five to forty school-age boys, spending time with the kids and working on an ambitious project to put a roof on an addition to the home which would house visiting mission teams.

Why Jamaica, and why Sunbeam? It was a relatively short and thus, inexpensive, flight to Jamaica from our nearest airport, Minneapolis-St. Paul International Airport, about four and a half hours. English is the primary language spoken in Jamaica, making verbal communication relatively easy. Also, while petty theft and other non-violent crimes were certainly prevalent in the larger urban areas, it was a relatively safe foreign country, at least at the time we began this journey. Sunbeam Children's Home had potable running water [most of the time], indoor plumbing [when the water worked], electricity, and beds [humble though they may be], all amenities which we could certainly live without. However, these amenities allowed us to bring a wider range of individuals of all ages who would have the basic needs covered for sleeping, cooking, and doing our work projects. Finally, other congregations had already established relationships with the home to which we would travel. It seemed like a perfect location to go do some good in the world.

In 1995, I was married and a busy mother of two busy teenagers, working full time and earning only two weeks of vacation each year. My kids were in band, sports, and a multitude of other things as was I, and I didn't feel it was necessarily fair to expect that my husband would take care of everything while I flew off to the Caribbean in the middle of the winter. I really could not afford to pay the price to take part, and I had no hands-on construction skills. But I loved children and I had a reputation for remaining calm in stressful or overwhelming situations. I had a heart for adventure, a love for the Lord, and I had dreamed of such an experience for much of my life, but never believed that it could or would ever become a reality.

I remember walking up to our pastor after the church service in which this opportunity was announced and asked, "Is it open to women?", thinking perhaps macho, hammer-wielding guys with construction skills, muscles, and leather tool belts might be preferred. After all, as an old Jamaican proverb states, *"Cow no ha' no business inna ha'se play"* (A cow has no business in horse play) (McLean, 241). Pastor Duane assured me that all would be welcome, and he encouraged me to think about it.

Believe me, there was no need to even think. But to save myself from appearing like an over-excited twelve-year-old, I calmly thanked my pastor and went home after church, my head spinning. I felt a nudge, sensing immediately that God was telling me I needed to do this. And it happened.

The very next year, despite an overwhelming desire to return, I felt I could not afford to go to Jamaica again. But, given my organizational skills and the passion for this mission that had taken hold of me after the first year, I was asked in Year Three if I would be interested in being the mission team leader and coordinate all the details of the mission. I took on that role like I take on most of the important things in my life: with passion, determination, and large amounts of organizational fortitude. I served as coordinator of those Jamaica missions for a period of years until I felt it was time to take a break and turn it over to our current, very capable leaders.

Lessons Learned in Jamaica is compilation of stories of my short-term mission experiences in Jamaica and the lessons that those experiences have taught me. Each chapter focuses on a specific lesson. These stories center mostly on Sunbeam Children's Home, our home base and the heart of our efforts, but also include memories created by visiting other children's homes, nurseries, schools, facilities for the aged or developmentally disabled, and many other organizations in Jamaica which I had the opportunity to visit over the years. The stories reflect experiences that are deeply personal to me, and these stories would have been written whether or not it resulted in the publication of a book to share with others. They are written in the first person in an informal, conversational style, as if you are listening to me speak. The words are sometimes lifted directly from journals and notes written by me at the time. Documenting these experiences in this way provides me with a place to escape and reflect on things that have turned me into the person I am today. These Jamaica experiences and the lessons they have taught me are an important part of my life.

The stories reflect my own perspective, as well as the activities of my own church's mission teams. The experiences of other mission groups could be very different. In many cases, I have changed the names of either team members or the Sunbeam boys to protect their privacy; other times, I used real names, but never last names. At any rate, the names are but a minor consideration. In all cases, the stories and the lessons remain. Many of the stories are from the early years of mission trips, 1995 to the mid-2000s, from which I had an abundance of detailed notes and journals as leader and coordinator, though many reflections occurred beyond that timeframe, also. The country itself has changed a lot in those twenty five years, and it should not be assumed that the Sunbeam Children's Home, or Jamaica itself, are the same now as they are reflected in the stories. The beautiful thing, however, is that the lessons remain.

With more reliable funding, a larger and more qualified staff has made a difference in the lives of the Sunbeam boys. Approximately fifteen churches now send teams to this boys' home. These factors have all resulted in Sunbeam's children having more stable and hopeful lives. The boys are fed three meals a day, have better access to health care, go to school, and have behavior goals and consequences. They live in a Christian setting, surrounded by compassion and a sense of hope for the future. A caring and capable superintendent is in place and has created, with the help of others, a positive environment for these boys.

The island of Jamaica has changed considerably from the first time I visited, becoming significantly more westernized, bringing with that change both the good and bad that come with modernization. Drugs and violence have intensified; gang activity is rampant in some parts of the country; unemployment is high. Third world conditions exist everywhere; yet Jamaica is not without modern characteristics. If one has only traveled to Sunbeam or to Jamaica in the past decade, some of the stories in this book may not resonate. Despite its changes, Jamaica remains a beautiful country full of beautiful, kind, talented people. I love it and always will.

During the span of time in which I was traveling to Jamaica, I returned to college in my forties to earn my master's degree in Rhetoric and Applied Writing. When choosing a topic for my thesis, I was inspired by my travels to write about Jamaican folklorist and author, Louis Bennett, affectionately known in Jamaica as "Miss Lou." Though my thesis focused on Miss Lou's poems, stories, and performances, the research I conducted for that thesis provided me with important information about Jamaican history and culture. This research was invaluable to my understanding of the Jamaica I saw each year in my travels, as well as eventually providing foundational material for this book. In this collection of stories, I have inserted historical context and references from my thesis research when it seemed appropriate to do so.

This is a book about lessons learned. My lesson-teachers have been my Jamaica boys and my mission teammates through the years, as well as our long-time Jamaican friends and random Jamaicans on the street and in the shops and taxis and churches. They shared themselves, their country, and their culture with me. I will always be grateful for these lessons Jamaica has taught me, and for the faith building and perspective widening that these short-term mission experiences have provided me. I have learned that, when I am in a third world country surrounded by unfamiliar situations, witnessing overwhelming poverty and hopelessness, with all the comforts and conveniences of my normal daily life taken away, lessons are more easily learned and so deeply felt. They stick.

Along this book-writing journey, I came upon a delightful book of Jamaican proverbs, written by Beresford McLean (Mill City Press, 2018). In it is a compendium of Jamaican wisdom, passed down from McLean's own family and others through the ages, in the form of proverbs. The proverbs are presented as we would hear them in Jamaica even now, written in Patois, the dialect of the common people. In those proverbs, I recognized the Jamaica that I love, and realized that many of them reinforce the lessons that my mission experiences have taught me. I have chosen to include several of those proverbs to help the reader better understand the culture, the humor, and the beliefs of the Jamaican people as I have come to know them.

One of these proverbs states, *Wha yeye muh see, heart nuh leap"* (What the eye does not see, the heart does not leap) (McLean, 337). This proverb perfectly describes my Jamaican experience. Before I was involved, I thought I knew a little about short-term missions, and I had some minimal knowledge about the country of Jamaica. But it was only when I experienced it firsthand that my eyes were opened, and my heart filled. Until I witnessed children living in poverty and was able to put names and faces to the third world conditions I saw in textbooks and in the news, I was not compelled to action.

Many thanks to all those who have answered my endless questions, sat down for interviews, helped me recall details, and inspired me in the process of writing these stories. I hope that my mission teammates through the years will find joy in remembering these stories. They are a special kind of family. And I owe so many thanks to my own family for giving me up during the times I traveled to Jamaica each year so that I could indulge in one of my greatest passions, and then for listening to me talk about my Jamaica boys endlessly upon my return. Thanks to Marcus Anderson, who helped our church initially become involved in this relationship with Sunbeam Children's Home. Thanks also to my friend, Pastor Duane Semmler, who accompanied us on that first trip and others, pastored my family through the years, and continues to actively support the boys at Sunbeam. Most of all, thank you to my dear Jamaica boys, who will live in my heart forever.

Chapter 2

Lesson: It's Not the Length of Time, but the Quality of the Time That Matters

Though the bulk of my Jamaican experiences occurred at Sunbeam Children's Home, an experience in 1995 while visiting Strathmore Children's Home near Spanishtown, Jamaica, affirmed that I had made the right decision when I said "yes" to the call to be a short-term missionary. The experience and what it taught me is so important that it needs to be mentioned first.

Strathmore Children's Home is a place dear to my heart. From the first time I walked through the place in 1995 on a quick tour stop after church, I was drawn to the children and to the place. It would have been easier to deny that immediate connection. The children sat on concrete floors or on plastic bowls used as toilets, rooms were dark, and many children ran through the home and property with ragged shirts and no pants. The stench of urine and mildew was pervasive. Water service came and went with no warning, toilets overflowed from misuse or overuse or lack of maintenance, and dirty, insanitary water flooded through the home regularly from these incidents. Severely handicapped children were warehoused into small, dark rooms to find their own means of comforting themselves and each other. Basic care necessities for children—Tylenol, cough medicine, Kleenex, toilet paper—were valuable commodities, generally not immediately available. Children played on gravel and concrete. This place punched me in the gut but gave me great insight into the short-term mission experience.

Based on that quick tour early in our stay in 1995, I decided that I wanted to return to Strathmore later that week to spend some time with the kids. I brought fellow missionaries Patsy, Scott and Sandy with plans to spend time with the kids, as well as to try to make their physical environment a little more pleasant. We painted some of the bedroom walls that were dirty, sad, and lifeless. In all fairness, scrubbing and painting the walls was not, and should not have been, a priority for the two staff members who worked there. They had their hands full just trying to take care of the children's basic needs, such as nourishment, shelter, and physical safety. Nonetheless, the rooms were dark and dirty, certainly not soothing or pleasant for the children.

Once our physical labor was completed for that day, we read books to the kids while sitting out in the yard on the concrete or on the wooden playground structure constructed by a former mission team from another church. We blew bubbles, shared treats, held, hugged, laughed, and tried not to cry. I saw only three toys at Strathmore that year, two broken plastic cups and a Barbie Doll body with no arms or legs. Children played with rocks, sticks, and pieces of broken objects found in the trash or on the street. There were many children there on that day: Jason, Duane, Ainsley, Trisha, LaToya, Wayney, Scotteesha, and George, to name a few.

And there was Jonah.

I estimated Jonah to be about five or six years old. He had the most beautiful, engaging smile, and bright, sparkling eyes. He seemed oddly placed at this home. Strathmore was, and continues to be, a holding place for children before their court dates to determine a return to their homes or placement at another children's home. But the sad reality, at that point in its history, was that children often stayed at Strathmore for much longer periods of time, in some cases, several years. Their time to move on just never came. Many of Strathmore's children at that time were developmentally challenged in one way or another.

But little Jonah seemed different: able-bodied, alert, smart. He latched onto me immediately. In me, he found a person who touched him, hugged him, played with him, looked into his eyes, and smiled at him. Jonah was never far from my side that day. If I was ever to be found in a sitting position, he was on my lap. And if I had someone else on my lap, he skootched them over a little bit with his rear and parked himself next to them, so I then had two kids on my lap. Or maybe three. As I read stories, Jonah sat and put his hand on my arm, or on my leg, or around my neck—anywhere—as long as he was touching me. I patted him on the back, gently touched him on the face, and gave him lots of hugs. I did the things I did with my own children. I reached into my maternal bag of tricks and pulled out every little thing I could think of to let this bright, handsome little boy feel like he had a mommy for a day. I did these same things with many of the other children, as well, but it was Jonah who responded most outwardly. As I walked around, he reached up and held my hand. He declared himself my best friend. He didn't say much initially. But he smiled a lot.

When our driver returned and it was time for us to leave Strathmore at the end of the workday, Jonah held my one hand tightly with both his small hands, realizing I would soon be leaving. The agony of our upcoming good-bye was painfully clear on his face and in his body language. I am sure that he was thinking the same thing that I was: Why couldn't this day go on forever?

I gave Jonah a hug, the kind where his skinny little body was completely enveloped in my arms and his head tightly held against me. He hung on for dear life, as if he was begging me not to leave. I discretely tucked a Tootsie Roll into one grimy little hand and a Matchbox car in the other, told him to put them in his pocket, and I got into the waiting car. As I looked over the sea of little brown humans who had gathered to see us off, many of the children had tears in their eyes, but I was struck by the number who did not outwardly cry. Their sadness and need for comforting were obvious, but in the course of their young lives, they had learned the saddest lessons of all: one, people do not respond when you cry; and two, people don't come back. Even if they said they'd come back, they just didn't. It was in that moment that I knew that I would be back to Strathmore, again and again. I wasn't sure there was anything I could do to change these children's lives, but I could come back. I knew that I could rally up the internal fortitude to look past the odors, the intense emotions, the dirty physical environment, and the discomfort of it all, and simply be present.

Flash forward to two years from that initial visit. During my second mission trip to Jamaica, I could not wait to return to Strathmore, as I had felt the pull since I left on that day two years prior. The image of Jonah was seared into my memory. It still is today, more than twenty-five years later. Once again, I had convinced a few of my fellow missionaries to accompany me for a day at Strathmore. It was not easy to get volunteers, and I didn't blame anybody for being uncomfortable at such a place; a day at Strathmore is a tough day. But there was never a doubt that I would find a way to visit, so we hired a driver and he delivered me and three others after a half-hour drive from our home base at Sunbeam Children's Home.

I got out of the car outside the Strathmore gate. The children did not know we were coming, so, one by one they appeared from behind corners, from inside of the building, and from the school room. Seeing our white faces, they looked curious and a bit wary. I took a deep breath, steeling myself for what I knew lay ahead, and opened the gate and walked through. I sensed that my partners were relying on me to lead the way, so I led them in, feeling like I needed to be the strong, confident one. I was neither, but I faked it. Then, a little boy with a big, bright smile came out to greet me. He grabbed both of his hands into mine, just as he had done two years earlier, and he said, before I even had a chance to say anything, "Miss Eidi! You come back!"

It was Jonah.

I had spent approximately six hours with this little boy two years prior. Two years! For two entire years, he kept in his memory the joy that he felt when I had held his hand, touched his face, and gave him the attention that he deserved. Maybe he remembered the Tootsie Roll and the Matchbox car. I choose to believe that the joy that he felt on that day two years prior had gotten him through the inevitable challenges that he would have endured on a regular basis: hunger, loneliness, sadness, hopelessness, fear. This was my moment of recognition regarding the value of short-term missions. We *can* make a difference in a short period of time. And it was in this moment of recognition that I understood why I would continue my own involvement in Jamaica's children's homes, as well as talk to others about it. After all, *"Likkle pepper bun big man mouth"* (A little pepper burns a big man's mouth) (McLean, 95). Small things can have a huge impact. And we all can do small things.

I do not know what became of Jonah. He was not a Strathmore the next time I returned, and the staff member on duty there did not know where he had been placed. How I wish I could find Jonah today and tell him that the five words he spoke to me, "Miss Heidi, you come back!" changed my life.

In 2005, I had the privilege of meeting Michael, age fifteen, at Sunbeam Children's Home. During the time that our team was at Sunbeam, Michael ran away. Back in the day, it happened with the boys now and then. Thankfully, he returned after a few days. I was drawn to Michael and he to me, and I spent quite a bit of time in one-on-one conversations with him that week. That year, I was the leader of the mission team and had to take care of such things as exchanging our American money for Jamaican Dollars at the local bank, as well as going out into the community for needed supplies. One day, I asked Michael if he would be my bodyguard when I went to the bank in Old

Harbour, as well as when I walked to Gutter's Corner to buy various work project supplies and food items for the team.

Michael told me that, for as long as he could remember, he lived at the marketplace in Spanishtown. At age fifteen, he could not remember ever living with a family in a house, so he had literally been living on the street his entire life, or at least for as long as his memory spanned. The marketplace in Spanishtown is a large town square area in the center of town in which vendors sell their wares such as fruits and vegetables, sugar cane, newspapers, clothing, and household items such as brooms and brushes and plastic tubs. This was Michael's home. He would either beg or steal food from the various vendors, and sleep wherever he could find a place he perceived to be safe.

One of the female vendors gave him food when she could, and was the only person that Michael really had in the world. Ironically, she was the person who eventually reported him to the police to get him some help. Michael was extremely hurt that the one person he trusted had, in his eyes, betrayed him. He was turned over to Jamaica Children's Services and eventually placed at Sunbeam Children's Home sometime in the months prior to our team's arrival.

At Sunbeam, Michael felt lost and had not yet developed any significant connections among the other boys. I worked hard to gain his trust, taking every opportunity I could to encourage him to talk, and to look into his eyes and listen intently. One evening, Michael told me, with tears in his eyes, "I have no one." He did admit that living at Sunbeam at least provided him with food, a bed, and the ability to go to school. But he struggled daily, even hourly. And I struggled to find the words to encourage and support him. All I had was a listening ear, the ability to comfortably ask God for help, and my maternal instinct. But I made Michael a priority that week.

Later that week, our departure from Sunbeam was drawing near. Michael took me aside the night before we were to depart. We sat down next to each other on the top step of the stairs leading downstairs. He put his arm around me and thanked me. He said, in such a mature, articulate manner, "I am going to try. I know this is the best place for me right now. Thank you for listening to me and being my friend, Miss Eidi. I will miss you." I know he had thought long and hard about what to say, and it was from his heart.

We struggle, as short-term missionaries, to make a difference in a short amount of time. For all I know, Michael could have reverted to despondency a week later; all I was able to later learn is that he did stick around, and there were no more run-away incidents. I will have to be content knowing that I gave it a try and that he was one day comfortable with the structure, discipline, and camaraderie of the Sunbeam Children's Home family.

In the world of short-term missions, it is not uncommon to hear, "Why do you bother? You cannot change the world! No matter what you do, it is not going to change the world these kids live in!" For many people, all it takes to move forward is to hear "It is impossible." I might be one of those.

The world is full of those who discourage rather than encourage. If we listen to those discouragers, not much would be accomplished. And a lot of little boys in Jamaica would not have experienced a full stomach, a clean school uniform, a comfortable mattress to sleep on, and hope for a better future. And a lot of adults and young people from Minnesota would not have seen a third world country, listened to the words of a scared and hopeless boy, ironed his school uniform, cooked him a hearty meal, or provided a safe haven when he was scared and lonely. They would not have had a perspective-changing experience, grown in their faith, and known the loyalty, the friendliness, and the beauty of the Jamaican people.

I defy anyone to tell me that I cannot at least *help* change the world, one child at a time. If we truly believe that God has called us for a particular purpose, we persevere. We keep returning, we keep moving forward, even though many times it means one step forward and two steps back, or three, or four. Do we do it alone? Of course not. But as Mother Teresa once said, "*I alone cannot change the world. But I can cast a stone across the waters to create many ripples."*

We also hear, in short-term missions, or long-term missions for that matter, "Why go to another country? There are plenty of children in our country that could use our help." The answer I have formulated over many years is that God does not discriminate. All children are equal in his eyes. All children, no matter where they live, deserve food, water, love, attention, and a chance to have dreams for the future and live to adulthood. Many churches, including my own, have mission programs focused on children in the local or regional area in addition to those focused on Jamaica or other foreign countries. All share the common goal to spread God's love by performing ministries of service to those who might need it. At home or abroad, God does not place more value in a child from either place. I don't either.

On my very first visit to Sunbeam Children's Home in 1995, another moment in time played a large part in my desire to return to Jamaica again and again. The boys were lined up for their evening meal, a practice designed to maintain order and avoid mass chaos while serving the boys their plates before they sat down for their meals. With just a fleeting thought as I looked at the line-up of boys, I pictured my own two children, standing randomly in that row of skinny little Jamaican boys. But for the grace of God, my children could have been part of that line-up of barefoot children. They could have hungry tummies, been abandoned by a parent who abused them, lived in an insecure environment, or faced an unsure future. Placing my children in that line-up shook me to the core. My two beautiful children were instead born into a privileged world. What I knew about my own children then: that they embraced love and hugs and attention; that they sometimes needed us to be close when they went to bed so they could go to sleep; that they would get a fever or a stomachache or needed medical care, or that they just needed Mama's touch. My children would have not gotten those things where I was standing at that moment in Jamaica. They just would have had to tough it out and hope for a better day tomorrow.

Pastor Corey wrote a touching story in the church newsletter shortly after his return from Jamaica in 2003, about how he was raised as "another man's son" when his birth father left his mother and his mother remarried. He wrote, "Sunbeam Children's Home exists to take responsibility for 'another man's son'. It exists to shoulder burdens others cannot. Third world countries riddled with poverty need men and women who are willing to take responsibility for others, until those needing care can care for themselves. This is our challenge! *As Christians, we do not have the privilege to idly stand by while others perish. The Bible is clear about our role in taking care of others*" (emphasis mine).

Freedom of worship is guaranteed by the Jamaican constitution. I once heard, though without documented evidence, that Jamaica has more churches per capita than any other nation. Most Jamaicans are Protestant, with the largest denomination being Church of God, consisting of various Protestant denominations that all use his name, followed by Seventh Day Adventist, Pentecostal, and Baptist. Contrary to popular belief, less than one percent of people living in Jamaica are Rastafarians. We have, for the most part, felt welcome and appreciated in our travels there, and faithfulness is generally respected. It makes Jamaica a good place for us to carry out our activities at Sunbeam and beyond.

God does not ask us to do heroic deeds, just the simple things, to stretch further than we otherwise might do so comfortably. And so, we do the simple things: develop relationships with the children, try to give them some good days, and make physical improvements to their living environment. "Why do you bother?", some ask. I bothered—all of us bothered—because that is indeed how we change the world: one child at a time. I will never, ever doubt the value of my church's influence on the lives of the boys of Sunbeam, and many of those boys, now adults, have told us so. I love my church for its commitment to this ministry.

So many mission groups that come to Jamaica, or to any other mission location around the world for that matter, stay in a hotel or a church, and go out for the morning or afternoon and work on a project at a school or orphanage or elsewhere in the community, and then spend the rest of the day doing other tourist activities. Sometimes their situations necessitate this approach, and I am not being critical. This is something that may be necessary due to capacity or accessibility or security concerns, for example. But the foresight of the very early mission groups to Sunbeam and of Rev. Cedric Lue, who founded Sunbeam Children's Home, was to have mission teams stay right at the boys' home. I am calling this "immersion ministry." Our first major project was to help construct a large addition in the back of the Sunbeam building, to make this immersion ministry possible. The building addition housed large, open men's and women's dorms, with bathrooms and showers in each. These living quarters have been used ever since that time for visiting mission teams.

This immersion creates a truly meaningful experience, as the missionaries live in the same physical conditions as the people they are helping. It has truly been an enriched and enlightening experience for us to sleep under the same roof, share meals, and witness firsthand the ebbs and flows of our boys' days. By understanding them better, we can help them better.

Rev. Lue, Sunbeam's founder, was a native Jamaican of Chinese ancestry. Many Chinese people were brought to Jamaica as slave laborers on the sugar plantations once the African slave population had decreased. Dr. Lue and his wife together were the initial directors of Sunbeam. Pastor Lue's inspiration for starting the boys' home came in 1974 as he read *The Cross and the Switchblade.* This book was written by David Wilkerson, a country preacher who felt called to travel to the heart of New York City in the late 1950s and early 60s to bring the gospel to the violent street gangs. It is easy to see how such a story of courage, resilience, and faith would inspire Pastor Lue to allow God to use him to do the impossible: to save those young children in Jamaica whom many think were beyond saving or perhaps not worthy of saving.

The boys' home was first located in the town of Mandeville, about thirty-five miles west of its current location. At the time, the roads were very poor and frequently flooded. It was difficult to get to and from Mandeville. So, Pastor Lue was able to purchase a new property just east of Old Harbour near Gutter's Corner, Sunbeam's current location. He liked this new property because it had about five acres of agricultural land on which crops could be grown to feed the boys as well as to provide a means of teaching responsibility to the boys through working the farm. At the time Pastor Lue purchased the property, it was planted with three acres of corn, vegetables, peas, pumpkin, as well as a variety of fruit trees. There was also plenty of room to raise pigs, chickens, and goats. The building we now know as Sunbeam Children's Home had been built only five years prior to our church's first visit there in 1995. We owe a debt of gratitude to Pastor Lue for laying the groundwork for the ministry we have there today.

If we travel to Sunbeam Children's Home and do one little thing that truly makes an impact on the life of even one of the boys, our trip will not have been in vain. It reminds me of the [paraphrased] starfish story, originally from Loren Eiseley's 1969 essay entitled "The Star Thrower":

One day, an old man was walking along a beach that was littered with thousands of starfish that had been washed ashore by the high tide. As he walked, he came upon a young boy who was determinedly throwing the starfish back into the ocean, one by one. Perplexed by what he saw, the man looked at the boy and asked him what he was doing. Without looking up from his task, the boy replied, "I'm saving these starfish." The old man chuckled out loud and said, "Son, there are thousands of starfish and only one of you. What difference can you make?" The boy picked up a starfish, tossed it into the water and said, "I made a difference to that one!"

"That one" may have been Omar or Davean or Richard or Glendon or Junior or Franseco or Damien or hundreds of other Jamaican boys we have come to know and love over the years.

Chapter 3

Lesson: Sewing is a Ministry. Laundry is a Ministry. Anything can be a Ministry.

Our sewing ministry began, for the most part, in 1998, when our team arrived after a period of several months in which Sunbeam employed no dedicated laundry person. Other staff members did what they could, but there were piles and piles of dirty laundry and clothes in various states of disrepair. Many boys were forced to stay home from school because they had no uniform that was clean or in good repair, a requirement for school attendance. One of our many work projects for our visit that year was to simply reduce the laundry build-up, as well as repair as many articles of clothing as we could.

Teammates Shirley and Kathy spent most of the week doing whatever it took to repair and clean these uniforms. My mother, a seamstress herself, had sent along as a donation, lots of khaki-colored fabric, the color of the boys' school uniforms, as well as buttons, thread, zippers, and other sewing supplies. Others were equally as generous, as they were year after year in providing us with money or donations to help us with our work projects. I remember how overwhelmed Shirley felt when she initially saw the pile of uniforms that needed repair. But one by one, she worked her way through the uniforms realizing that, with every little fix, it was another little boy who would proudly be on his way to school with a fresh uniform. Shirley and Kathy had a system: Shirley ripped out the zipper, pinned in a new one and sewed on the buttons. Kathy took it from there and sewed in the zippers on the old White sewing machine.

O'Neil, a sixteen-year-old at Sunbeam, became an expert at threading the sewing machine, rethreading the bobbin, and troubleshooting when there were problems. Like a loyal puppy, he happily sat next to our seamstresses day after day, eagerly awaiting his next opportunity to help. He particularly enjoyed running the foot feed.

This was the year that we found out rather quickly that many of the clothes the kids were wearing were beyond repair. We discretely made a pile, brought the items to the garbage pit, and burned them with the other garbage. It sounds harsh, I know. We talked about it among ourselves and with the house staff beforehand, explaining that we would be careful to only dispose of those clothing items for which repair was not an option and for which we had brought replacements. If we would have just thrown them in the garbage pit and not burned them, we knew the kids would retrieve them and haul them back inside. We debated this issue back and forth because we did not want to disrespect the boys' meager possessions. Our concerns turned out to be unfounded when the boys proudly sported new clothes all week and quickly forgot about their ragged, older ones. Over the years, the clothing donations to the boys have increased a thousandfold. The boys do look and feel better about themselves with clothing, especially when the occasional Nike swoosh or New England Patriots or Buffalo Bills football jersey appears in the donated items.

Our sewing ministry grew by leaps and bounds once Cindy joined our team. Each year, Cindy brought her own sewing machine to

Jamaica as one of her two airline-allowed pieces of luggage and hauled it home again. She set up shop in Sunbeam's dining room all week, and the boys seemed to come out of the woodwork with items of clothing that needed repair. This happened every day we were there, all day long, and continues to occur each time we visit Sunbeam. It never occurred to me that a missionary's work would include repairing a blown-out crotch in a pair of pants, replacing a zipper, or sewing buttons on school uniforms but, of course it can, and in our case, it does.

Over the many years in which our sewing ministry was in full swing, I observed how the boys gravitated toward Cindy and our other seamstresses, and the interaction that would occur as they were repairing the boys' clothes. Cindy and the boys, sitting together and sharing stories, talked about what the boys learned in school that day, what they wanted to be when they grew up, laughing, talking about life. These boys had so little to call their own but entrusted their very few prized clothing possessions to Cindy to fix or embellish. They willingly became open and vulnerable with their life stories, their fears, and their dreams. One year, in addition to every conceivable clothing repair, some of the boys had the idea that they wanted zippers in the bottom of their jeans. So, of course Cindy catered to their little fashion whims. Zippers it was! One year they wanted Michael Jackson-like gloves. So, they got gloves. When skinny jeans became a thing, the boys wanted their school uniform slacks made skinnier. The superintendent put the kibosh on that one.

The boys craved this intimacy with maternal figures, as most children do, but in the case of our Jamaica boys, it perhaps reminded them of the kind of relationship they had, or at least dreamed of having, with their mother or their grandmother. As I look back on photos of Cindy's sewing ministry, I see the boys laughing, leaning in, sitting as close to Cindy as they can get, *connecting*. It's an important ministry. Sewing is a ministry. Anything we do at the boys' home is a ministry. It's part of being a missionary.

It seems that the average person thinks that being a missionary means standing on a street corner passing out Bibles, quoting scripture, and converting the natives. If that what it means, seriously I would be a dreadful missionary. But being a missionary is sewing on buttons. It is repairing toilets, replacing screens, planting tomatoes, building a chicken coop, giving a hug, or doing the laundry.

In 1998, I journaled about helping the staff with laundry. A new staff member, Mrs. Chambers, had just begun employment at Sunbeam that very day, and she had high standards. Team member Lori reported at our team meeting on the first evening that she had already been fired once. When we arrived at the beginning of the week, there were piles and piles of dirty and in many cases, musty and moldy, clothes. Many were in very bad condition. With the lack of a laundress, the laundry had not been kept up with for an entire year and, as mentioned previously, some kids had not been able to go to school because they didn't have clean uniforms in good repair. And the bedsheets in the home had not been washed for months.

We had sought donations back in Minnesota and brought along several single sheets for the boys' bunks and suitcases full of clothing for the boys. Think about the fact that this is a home in which forty boys live. Do you know any boys? Did you raise any boys? You know how dirty they get, and the rate at which the laundry piles up with only a few boys in the house. Boys get dirty. Now think of bedsheets. Most boys at Sunbeam just slept on a bottom sheet tucked into a mattress, if they even had a sheet. That's forty sheets. The boys slept in whatever clothes they had, however long they had been wearing them, regardless of the outside activities they had taken part in. Hopefully, one begins to understand the magnitude of the situation we encountered that year. We had two team members working nearly full-time that week helping with the laundry situation, and several others pitching in now and then.

Marisa and Lori were sweating to keep up with Mrs. Chambers. Mrs. Chambers inspected what had been washed by our team members and hung up on the line, and if it did not meet her specifications, back it went through the wash, where she expected all stains to be removed. She had high standards but was also infinitely grateful for our help. Mrs. Chambers used a blue bar of *Bomber* soap to scrub the clothes by hand, brushed them with a wire brush, put them in one of the two concrete sinks to soak, and on they went into the old wringer washing machine, which had long since lost its wringer. This was before the day that Ole and Bill went in to Spanishtown and brought home a shiny new automatic washer. The three of them washed all day, every day, for five days, and indeed got caught up on every single piece of laundry. Of course, as we all know, laundry is a never-ending job and multiplies at the speed of light, but for one moment in time it was caught up. Each numbered box in the laundry distribution room had a few items of clean clothing, each boy had a clean bedsheet to sleep on, and school uniforms were repaired, cleaned, pressed, and school-ready!

I will never forget the day in 1998 when I looked out in the back yard to see a large open bed truck with a shiny new commercial-quality washing machine strapped in the back. We had sent Ole, Bill, and Mrs. Lue out shopping, with the goal of finding a washing machine that could be delivered immediately. Mrs. Lue preferred a wringer washer, but they simply were not made anymore, so such a purchase was out of the question. With our team money, we purchased this machine for 800 American Dollars. As the team leader, I admit some fear of our $800 fancy shmancy machine breaking immediately and sitting there unused, or the more likely scenario: Mrs. Chambers just being more comfortable doing things the old way, by hand. But I had to trust that we had done the right thing, and sure enough, after our team handyman Charlie got the washer hooked up and gave a little tutorial, Mrs. Chambers felt comfortable enough to use the new machine and had proudly begun to wash a load of laundry.

Typically, to participate in this short-term mission experience, each team member is required to pay about $1,000 to a fund managed by the coordinator of the trip. Out of that fund, all expenses for the Jamaica visit are paid including such things as airfare, meals, bus transportation on the island, and thousands of dollars for food and work project supplies, whether purchased prior to our departure from Minnesota or after we arrive in Jamaica. With the money each of us pays for this opportunity, as well as money earned in fundraising activities beforehand, we generally have a kitty to use for unforeseen requests such as this washing machine. The same sort of thing occurred during our 2018 trip, when the superintendent asked if we might be willing to purchase a new refrigerator for the Sunbeam kitchen. A government inspection was coming up soon, and he was concerned that the current refrigerator would not meet the required specifications. We were able to buy a beautiful stainless-steel refrigerator-freezer combo and place it in the kitchen the same day. Purchasing this large appliance would have been a financial hardship for Sunbeam, and we were happy and proud to do this for our Jamaica family.

2014 was the year of the laundry for me personally and the beginning of a stepped-up laundry role each time I returned. Though I had always assumed the role of the laundress for team t-shirts in the middle of the week, in 2014 I spent most of the week at the concrete scrub sink, the washing machine, or the clothesline. Most trips since then I could be found doing the same thing. I like to call it my laundry ministry. I started early in the morning by finishing up what Miss Ivarene had left in the washing machine or on the clothesline the night before, as well as daily team laundry. It involved washing a few loads in the automatic washer—which took approximately forty-five minutes to fill with water each cycle due to the low water pressure—scrubbing by hand, hanging on the line, and folding. Hanging clothes was a challenge in many ways but primarily because clothespins were a rarity. They were constantly disappearing or breaking, so it became a regular thing to bring more with us each year in our suitcases.

When Miss Ivarene arrived at ten o'clock in the morning, I helped her scrub, hang, and fold, being a little more vigilant in her presence to do exactly as she did so that she did not to feel as though she needed to re-do everything I had helped her with. The greatest benefit to me?

Those laundry days, my laundry mission, provided hours and hours of conversation with Miss Ivarene, and at least a few of the boys, who loved helping us with our projects.

As of 2020, Miss Ivarene had been with Sunbeam for about twenty years. She comes to work each weekday at ten o'clock in the morning and stays until mid-afternoon. The laundry operation is housed in an outside lean-to addition in the back of the Sunbeam building. It is perhaps ten feet by ten feet in size. It houses two automatic washers, a double concrete sink, some large sorting bins, and some clotheslines for hanging clothing when there is no room to be hung outside. The outside clotheslines hang over a dirty area that is infested with ants. As a visitor hanging laundry, I learned over the years to never wear flip flops or sandals on laundry duty. Tennis shoes and a healthy shot of insect repellant are the only way to survive the task without spending the next night itching ant bites all night.

As mentioned, just filling the automatic washers with water is quite a task. The washers are then overstuffed due to the sheer volume of clothing. The wear and tear on the machines is significant with their heavy use, the lack of proper care and maintenance, and the extreme weather conditions. It is not unusual for one or both automatic machines to be out of commission for some period of time until someone with appliance repair or plumbing knowledge shows up. That could be days, months, or longer. In Jamaica, its people have learned that *"Kitchen claat tun table claat"* (A kitchen/dish cloth turns into a tablecloth) (McLean, 38). You do the best you can with the resources you have. It's a simple as that.

Every boy must wear a school uniform to school each day, from the primary grades through high school. The color of each level of uniform is determined by the parish in which the child lives. The boys' uniforms for most primary schools consists of a khaki-colored, short-sleeved, button-down shirt with matching khaki-colored slacks, a belt, and dress shoes. No tennis shoes, sandals, or flip flops are allowed. Girls wear a particular color of skirt, again determined by the parish in which she lives, often with a white or gingham blouse. Most of the high schools require boys to wear a white shirt, tie, and dress slacks (no blue jeans) instead of khaki.

Miss Ivarene's clothing distribution room was built in the last decade and sits at ground level below the overhang of the visitor dorms in the back of the building. It is dark and damp, lit by one light bulb. There is a cubby system in which there is a space for each boy, or if that system has become disorganized, cubbies for various sizes. Additionally, there are hanging rods on which multiple school uniforms hang. An ironing board and a well-worn chair occupy the remaining floor space in the small room. Additionally, there is generally an ironing board set up in the dining room or main living area of the home, and some of the boys take it upon themselves to wash and iron their own uniforms so they can assure they get the same one back. Others, especially the younger ones, use a uniform out of the general uniform inventory.

One year, I promised Miss Ivarene that I would send her a big box of wire hangers when I got home to Minnesota, and I did so. It continues to amaze me how needy they are for things that are so expected and taken for granted by us. Imagine having school uniforms for forty boys, scrubbing them all by hand and ironing them all, then having no hangers to hang them up so they still look nice the next day. Nothing is easy.

Some might consider sewing and laundry to be "women's work," and in Jamaica, it is. However, in the matriarchal Jamaican culture, the role of women extends far beyond traditional women's tasks like sewing and laundry and cooking. Women tend to pay a dominant role in society as heads of households. This is an extension of Jamaica's colonial history. Perhaps a short Jamaica history lesson would help put the role of Jamaican women in context. As is the case in the United States, Jamaica was originally inhabited by a native Amerindian population, in Jamaica's case, the Arawaks, when "discovered" by Christopher Columbus in 1494. The original Arawak population numbered approximately 60,000. By 1509, Jamaica was occupied by Spain, which established sugar plantations on the island, using the native Arawaks as slave laborers. In the passing of only one hundred years, the Arawak population had been destroyed by conflict and disease, causing the Spaniards to seek laborers elsewhere.

In 1670, after a period of Spanish ownership, Jamaica became a possession of England. The importation of West African slaves to Jamaica by England began in the early seventeenth century to fulfill the need for labor to drive Jamaica's plantation economy. The slave population grew fast in the early seventeenth century and the ratio of black to white on the island became approximately fifteen to one. The prosperity of the island at that time can be attributed in great part to the exploitation of the slave laborers, a situation that persisted for nearly two hundred years until slavery was abolished in 1834.

Once the importation of West Africans to Jamaica began to slow, a significant number of East Indian and Chinese people were shipped to Jamaica to replenish the labor supply on the sugar plantations. In smaller numbers were Europeans and Middle Easterners. As a result, the population of Jamaica today consists of a variety of races and nationalities, many of whom have intermarried and created a vibrant cultural mix of religions, philosophies, music, folklore, traditions, and literature. Hence, the nation's motto, *Out of many, One People.* Though some critics chide this motto as idealistic, it does represent the nature of modern Jamaica, a mixture of races and cultures, though predominantly those of African descent. Jamaica remained a British colony until 1962, when Jamaica became an independent nation and a member of the British Commonwealth.

The slave family in the New World, particularly when the slave population was almost exclusively from Africa, was indeed matriarchal in nature (Lawrence, *Women* 4) and this can be traced to the importance of women in the African cultures from which many of the enslaved Africans descended. Lawrence calls the resulting matriarchal family of the Caribbean slave society "a synthesis of an African cultural survival with the realities of slavery in the area" (4). In many West

African cultures, the woman lived with her children in one dwelling and her male partner lived in a separate dwelling. Each wife took turns cooking and sleeping with the man, and the children spent nearly all their time with their mother, developing a closer bond with her than with their father. Marriage was not sanctioned or required by any state or religious body. Rather, it involved a consensual relationship between the families involved (Lawrence, *Women* 3). This situation required creativity and resourcefulness, a characteristic that has prevailed throughout the history of Jamaican women. Merle Hodge, a Trinidadian critic and author, writes that "[in the New World], the function of fatherhood was limited to fertilizing the female. Gone was the status of head of family, for there was no family, no living in a unit with wife and children." (Merle Hodge, quoted in Lawrence, *Women* 3). Though it certainly doesn't apply to all Jamaican families, this history makes it easy to understand how modern Jamaica, though becoming increasingly westernized, still carries this matriarchal legacy.

"Women's Work." It has a negative connotation in our country. But while in Jamaica, our female mission team members do their best to relieve the workload of the female staff members—cooks, laundress, house mothers—and to the best of our abilities, stand in as mother, sister, and grandmother figures for the boys. Sewing is a ministry. Cooking is a ministry. Laundry is a ministry. Mothering is a ministry. Every Christian, no matter who they are or what they do, are called to minister to others. We are ministering to our Jamaica boys and in the process, living our faith. *"Truly I tell you, whatever you did for one of the least of these brothers and sisters of mine, you did for me." (Matt. 25:40)*

Chapter 4

Lesson: Prepare, Then Leave the Rest to God

As one might imagine, preparation for a short-term mission trip for fifteen to twenty people to a third world country requires a lot of planning, to assure the enjoyment, efficiency, and safety of the participants and activities. There is a Jamaican proverb that reads, *Bucket wid 'ole a battam nuh ha nuh business a ribaside"* (A bucket with a hole in its bottom has no business at a riverside) (McLean, 18). Simply stated, one must be prepared for the task at hand. Likewise, *"Pudden cyaa bake widout fiah* (Pudding cannot bake without a fire) (McLean, 40). One learns quickly, however, that despite the best laid plans and preparations—plugging the hole in the bucket or building a fire prior to making pudding—traveling into this kind of environment requires a bit of flexibility. A cool head helps, as well as the ability to punt. Adopting the Jamaican *"No Problem, Mon"* is a really good idea.

As we arrived in Montego Bay in January 2000, we were greeted, as we always are, over the loudspeaker after our plane touched down on the tarmac. We were welcomed to Jamaica, given some basic instructions about the required process we were to follow through Customs and Immigration, and were told, *"We want to inform you that forty-six pieces of luggage were unfortunately left behind in Minneapolis because there was too much weight on the plane."* We were left to wonder, were any of them in our group's forty-two bags and boxes? What if some of our critical supplies did not make it? The electric drill? Someone's work boots? Our clothing and shoe donations for the boys? Critical ingredients for our meals? Or, heaven forbid, the toilet paper? We did not know, until we collected our bags in the Montego Bay Baggage Claim area and took inventory, that every one of our forty-two fifty-pound suitcases and boxes had safely arrived, including two computer monitors and several boxes of medical supplies. They had not made it through Customs yet, but at least we now knew that they had made it onto the plane and into Jamaica. While I guess I should have been concerned for those unfortunate people to whom the other forty-six missing pieces of luggage belonged (and I'm quite sure our group's massive amount of luggage contributed to exceeding that plane's weight limit), I admit to a bit of a selfish mindset at that moment. As the leader of this group, I felt responsible for the well-being of twenty-one people, twenty-one carry-on bags, and forty-two pieces of luggage arriving simultaneously in the airport of a third world country. I said a silent prayer of thanks for this good fortune.

Due to the sheer volume of goods we bring in as donations and gifts to Sunbeam Children's Home, as well as tools, electronics, and other non-traditional items, getting it all through Customs and Immigration easily and efficiently is often a challenge. One of my favorite Customs memories is of Pastor Duane trying to talk his way through Customs with a suitcase full of brand-new donated tennis shoes for the kids, attempting to explain why he should not have to pay duty tax on them. He used his best persuasive techniques, but seemingly was no match for the seasoned female Customs Official, who was rapidly losing patience. Duane eventually had to resort to playing the "reverend" card, believing that the Customs official certainly wouldn't argue with a preacher, a Man of God, for heaven's sake. I think that poor Customs official finally just got a headache and gave up, flagging the Reverend and his suitcase full of sixteen brand new pairs of tennis shoes right on through, with no duty to pay.

Three Customs Lessons we have learned over the years: (1) Break up the large number of single, similar items. For example, if bringing forty rolls of toilet paper, put a few in each suitcase; (2) If bringing new, unused items, take them out of their original packaging and remove any price tags; and (3) If it is anticipated that items may raise eyebrows or invite trouble, like medical supplies, electronic items, or power tools, assign those suitcases to the more seasoned missionary veterans and put them at the very end of the Customs line. When those seasoned travelers finally get up to the counter, the Customs Officials are often so tired of dealing with the exasperating missionary group and their endless number of suitcases that they are more likely to just wave the annoying people through. And I'll add a fourth piece of advice: be respectful and kind but proceed quickly and confidently.

One way or another, we always manage to eventually get the entire group and all the luggage through Customs, some years easier and faster than others. One year, in addition to everything else, we brought with us a guitar amplifier and a weed eater. Customs officials put their heads together and spoke in hushed tones trying to figure out how to handle these strange items, and eventually called their supervisor. I mean really, what tourist brings a weed eater to Jamaica? And the year that we brought in computer monitors and two suitcases full of medications and medical equipment, we did eventually, with some begging and pleading and explaining, get through without losing our tempers or getting arrested. The trouble was to come later that day.

We are always met at the Montego Bay airport by our good friends, protectors, and guides, Pooh and Marla, and often various members of their family to help load or to drive an additional vehicle to accommodate our group's needs. Because we had a big group that year, we knew ahead of time that there would not be enough room in Pooh's bus for the team and all thirty-eight of the suitcases, plus all our individual carry-ons. So, all thirty-eight supply suitcases were packed into a minivan driven by one of Pooh's sons. We packed up his cargo minivan from floor to ceiling and hopped on Pooh's bus with our personal carry-ons, for the four-hour trip across the island to Sunbeam Children's Home.

The van containing all our luggage and supplies made it no more than twenty miles before it broke down on the side of the road in the Jamaican countryside, presumably from the sheer weight of the cargo. Luckily, it had broken down near the country home of a local preacher, and he graciously allowed the van to be parked in his locked, gated driveway that night, with the understanding that Pooh and his son would come back the next day and tow it across the island to Sunbeam. We had no choice that night but to leave all our supplies, food, tools, and other valuable cargo in God's hands and take off to our destination. As it turned out, Pooh faithfully delivered the van and its cargo to us late the next day after a long, grueling trip for him as he towed the heavily laden van across the island on roads that can only be described by Americans as "challenging."

Driving in Jamaica is not for the faint of heart. Pooh is a master at navigating these roads, and most are paved, but many of the roads suffer from inadequate signage and inadequate maintenance and repair such as large potholes. Roads are often narrow and hug the edges of cliffs, canyons, forests, and mountainsides. Drivers often compete for road space with roadside vendors, other vehicles, pedestrians, bicyclists, chickens, and wandering goats. Roads in rural areas and near major tourist resorts are often heavily traveled and speeds are high. An elaborate system of horn honking is a secret language understood by only those who are frequent travelers on Jamaican roads, a system none of us have figured out yet but that Pooh, as a professional driver, is a master. It is across these roads that our faithful drivers were able to tow our ailing minivan full of essentials and arrive safely at Sunbeam. It was an unplanned and unpleasant turn of events after so much careful planning, but it worked out in the end and we were so grateful for

Pooh, as we have been so many times.

One of our favorite places to go on our pilgrimage day is Lime Cay, a small, uninhabited island a few miles out to sea from Port Royal, near Kingston, but it does require a bit of trust and well-placed prayers. More is written about our pilgrimage days in Chapter 9. Lime Cay is only 415 yards long (think four football fields) and 87 yards wide but is the largest of many small cays off this coast. Lime Cay is uninhabitable because it is occasionally submerged when the tide comes in; luckily, our group never witnessed this firsthand. The cay is about half wooded and the remainder, sand and coral, the latter being the magnet for tourists and on Sundays, the locals.

Lime Cay is accessed by traveling in old wooden boats taking off from Port Royal. The boats have the appearance of being a bit rickety, but at least the occupants are provided lifejackets. These boats bounce over the big waves of Port Royal Harbor, taking approximately twenty to thirty minutes out to Lime Cay for the price of about twenty American Dollars per person per round trip. There are no facilities or amenities on the island, including no food or beverage vendors, restrooms, buildings, or electric power. Over the years, our group has traveled out to the island for a get-away on our pilgrimage day after a sometimes-stressful, busy, hot, emotional week at Sunbeam.

During our January 2003 mission trip, we had hired two locals to take us out to Lime Cay in two such wooden boats and to pick us up after a pre-determined number of hours. As was our practice, we agreed upon a price with the boat drivers, but purposely did not pay them ahead of time so that they would be motivated to come and pick us up and safely deliver us back to Port Royal to receive their payment. Fast forward several hours. The sun had set, and we had spent a wonderful and relaxing beach day, but no boats had yet arrived to pick us up. I may have started quietly humming the theme from "Gilligan's Island". I admit that, as the group's leader, I was a bit concerned.

We were not in a state of panic. We were in Jamaica, after all, where little emphasis is placed on being on time. And not long after dusk, about ninety minutes after the agreed-upon pick-up time, we saw two boats appear on the horizon. Our Rastafarian boat drivers, in good spirits and full of smiles, one smoking what appeared to be a joint, arrived. We then bounced over the waves back to our port of safety, laughing to our hearts' content, donning our faded orange lifejackets that appeared to be older than most of us and stunk like the dickens. No worries, Mon.

The surprises aren't finished just because we leave Jamaica, either. One of the teenagers on our mission team, I will call him Robert, was not aware that, as we were loading up the suitcases onto Pooh's bus in preparation for our Sunbeam departure, one of the local dogs lifted his leg on a suitcase and left his mark. That suitcase just happened to be Robert's carry-on bag.

We made it to the Minneapolis-St. Paul International Airport, to be processed back into the country. All was well until we arrived in the Immigration area. Drug sniffing dogs are present in this area, especially when there are flights coming in from places like Jamaica where illegal drug traffic has historically been a problem. The dogs are trained to walk among the people and the luggage and alert their handler if they sniff out something suspicious. As our group was being processed through Immigration I recall noticing, ahead of me in line, quite a commotion. One of the dogs, a German Shepherd, was whining, barking, and excitedly prancing around Robert and his bag. There was no doubt that he was alerting his handler that he had indeed found something "suspicious."

Young Robert, not a seasoned traveler at the time, was horrified and somewhat panicked as the armed, uniformed Immigration Officer stepped in and asked Robert to "please come with me." Sherry stepped forward to see what was going on and tried to intervene on Robert's behalf. The officer informed her, in rather direct language, that she needed to remove herself from the area. Robert was placed between two very large bodyguard-ish officials while he and his carry-on bag were thoroughly searched and scrutinized. It took a while to discover what had actually happened, and it all turned out fine in the end, but the situation reminded us that, despite our best planning efforts, things happen. You do what you can to prepare, you pray a lot, and then you leave the rest to God. A good life lesson.

Chapter 5

Lesson: Be Thankful for Every Sense

As we descend out of the sky and get closer and closer to the island of Jamaica, usually from the cold winter weather of Minnesota, the color of the sea turns a Caribbean aquamarine and coral reefs become more visible. We hear a voice with a wonderful Jamaican inflection come onto the public address system of the aircraft upon landing. The smell of the Caribbean breeze, the sight of tropical plant life, and the kiss of the breeze on our faces as the aircraft's doors are opened to the tarmac provide a feast for our Minnesota winter-logged senses.

It is pure pleasure to touch down in Montego Bay, or "Mo Bay" or "Bay" to the locals. There are two major airports in Jamaica, Donald F. Sangster Airport in Montego Bay, and Norman Manley International Airport in Jamaica's capital city, Kingston. Montego Bay is located on the northern coast and Kingston on the southern coast. Sunbeam Children's Home is closer to the southern coast. Our mission team started the tradition of flying into Montego Bay because of its location on the opposite side of the island from Sunbeam, providing the opportunity for the team to ride across the island and see more of the country. It allowed us the opportunity to get a taste of the real Jamaica and its people. We first traveled along the beautiful northern coast, then through Fern Gully and the rain forest, over the mountains, and through Spanishtown on the south side. In recent years, landing in Mo Bay has simply been a safer choice than Kingston. Though Jamaica has gradually become more and more westernized, third world conditions exist all over the country, and traveling in the country is a humbling and eye-opening experience. We have continued this tradition of flying into Mo Bay, with only a few exceptions, for the last twenty-five years.

Before our annual trip across the island and back was shortened by the construction of a new highway linking the northern and southern parts of the island, every trip to Sunbeam included the three-mile trip through Fern Gully. Once a riverbed with a series of cascading waterfalls, it is now a road. Just over one hundred years ago, an earthquake destroyed the riverbed, forming a rock gorge instead. A road was built over this gorge in 1907, twisting its way under a canopy of dense rainforest plants with flickers of light penetrating through the forest. As we drive through the winding road toward our destination, we take in its natural beauty. A jumble of jungle plants, including over three hundred varieties of ferns, banana trees, Blue Mahoe, and others, compete for the rays of sunshine that make their way down through the thick forest canopy. One can take in the thick, pungent smell of dense vegetation. Vendors sell their wares in small shacks built into the side of the canyon, sometimes calling out to moving buses to stop and buy their goods or take their photo. The vendors perk up as our bus of "whiteys" drives by, a potential bus full of American dollars that might soon be in their pockets. To us Minnesotans, it is a smorgasbord of delightful sights and sounds.

The road through Fern Gully, though special in its own way, is typical of a drive on many of the back roads on the island. In 1998, I wrote in my journal of the explosion of sights, sounds, and odors that one encounters on a bus ride through the narrow roads in Jamaica's back country. This is best experienced in a minibus at full speed, with the windows down. An assortment of locally understood horn honks gets us through many narrow curves, meeting cars and trucks and buses passing each other in a lane that really belonged to us, but somehow becomes the narrow path for an oncoming vehicle to squeeze through and barely avoid the front grill of our bus. How we avoided a head-on collision over the years is truly a tribute to the driving skills of our beloved Pooh.

On our way across the island on the first day, we often stop at *The Ultimate Jerk Center*, in the Jamaican countryside, to roust our bland Minnesota taste buds to the vibrant flavors of Jamaica. We order things like jerk pork, jerk chicken, rice and beans, bammy (a Jamaican flatbread made with grated cassava, dipped in coconut milk and fried until golden brown), and festival (a Jamaican dumpling made from either flour or cornmeal and deep-fried or boiled). American soft drinks are sometimes available, and of course Jamaican Red Stripe beer, but when in Jamaica we tend to indulge in such Jamaican soft drinks as Ting (grapefruit soda), Kola Champagne, or "Bigga" brand sodas, which come in such flavors as ginger, pineapple, grapefruit, orange, and cream soda. Newcomers tend to experience a bit of sticker shock at the posted prices of $1,000 or $800 per meal, posted in Jamaican Dollars.

The devaluation of the Jamaican Dollar against the U.S. Dollar has continually occurred since the inflation in the 1980s and 1990s, to the point where, in mid-2021, one U.S. Dollar was equal to about 146 Jamaican Dollars. So, it is not surprising that a meal at *The Ultimate Jerk Center* might cost $600 to $1000 Jamaican (~$4.00 to $8.00 U.S. Dollars). Though the Jamaican Dollar is divided into 100 cents just as in the United States, cent denominations were no longer used in Jamaica as of 2018. Products may be priced using cents but when one pays, the price is rounded to the nearest dollar.

The pulsating Reggae beat greets us at each settlement as we drive through the Jamaican towns, and particularly in Spanishtown as it is usually evening or even late night by the time we get to that part of the island. Evening to nighttime in the non-tourist areas of Jamaica is an amazing thing for a foreigner to witness. Vendors are out in the sidewalks and streets, selling everything from plastic laundry baskets to jerk chicken to sugar cane to fresh fish to newspapers. People, skinny dogs, pull carts, bicycles, goats, and chickens are everywhere. Cars and buses are honking, music is blaring. Exhaust fumes, fragrant flowers, body odor, dust, and gangi-induced shouts greet us as we drive by.

These odors to this day evoke a hodgepodge of emotions that include excitement, anticipation, awe, gratefulness, and profound happiness, with a pinch of anxiety, as we drive through Spanishtown and other smaller towns on our way to Sunbeam Children's Home. The most pervasive odor is that of smoke, a combination of marijuana, burning garbage, car exhaust, and pimiento wood smoke burning in metal drums used as ovens and grills for jerk chicken and jerk pork. In the early days of our Jamaica mission trips, we drove through the towns in the night air with the bus windows wide open so that we could feast on this smorgasbord of sights, sounds, and smells. Now, closed windows take precedence, primarily due to potential security concerns.

Once at Sunbeam, the sensory experiences continue. As the nightly team meeting is through and we are lying in our bunks in the dorm, I stop whatever thoughts may be going through my mind and allow myself the luxury of feeling a beautiful Caribbean breeze wafting through our sleeping area. I remember reading in a Jamaican novel a description of the night noises in our lives at home in the United States as being so very orderly: the hum of a furnace or air conditioner, the steady ticking of a clock, the running of the refrigerator. Lying in the women's dorm at night in Jamaica, I relish the disorderly sounds: barking dogs, crowing roosters, chirping crickets, croaking lizards, a car speeding by, hitting potholes on the road out front, the thumping bass of a stereo speaker in the distance. So many days begin simply by giving up the quest for sleep due to rooster or dog noise, but I never really mind while there. The dogs seemingly bark all night, with particular enthusiasm when wandering goats invade the garden or just pass through, or heaven forbid, the dogs manage to get into the fowl coop.

Perhaps my most indelible sound memory is that of a group of mourners gathered somewhere in the night, in the final stages of a three-day mourning period...singing and clapping, drums and bass rumbling, the unmistakable sounds of both anguish and praise, sung from the souls of the people that I have come to love so deeply. Their mourning comes from somewhere in the countryside, with no words or tune to be discerned. Despite the cacophony of unique sounds that I could lie and listen to for hours, I am often to sleep within moments. These sounds are my Jamaican lullaby.

Sights, sounds, and smells can evoke emotionally charged memories. Each year as I return to Jamaica and am cozily settled into my bunk, the first night sounds never fail to elicit a nostalgic, satisfying feeling. A study cited in 2010 by Rachel Rettner seems to explain what is happening. It suggests that "the same part of the brain that's in charge of processing our senses is also responsible, at least in part, for storing emotional memories. For instance, the smell of turkey could conjure up a smile as it reminds you of a joyful Thanksgiving, while the sound of a drill could make us shake in fear, since it may be linked to your last dental appointment." The study suggests that a particular sound is paired up with emotional information and stored in a specific part of the brain as a bundle, which then allows the sound to acquire an emotional meaning. My Jamaica night sounds will always evoke those positive vibes for me. That, and the smell of coffee, whose taste I despise, but whose smell gently transports me to childhood Christmas holidays at my grandmother's house.

Be thankful for every sense. Each one is a gift.

Chapter 6

Lesson: Celebrate the Ordinary

Seemingly ordinary things in our daily lives back home in Minnesota often translate to unique and unforgettable experiences when in Jamaica. Take the example of running to the store for ice cream. In Minnesota: grab your purse or wallet, get in your car, drive to the local Rainbow Foods, whip out the credit card and pay for the ice cream, drive home. Joyfully eat. In Jamaica: Guess at the cost and get some team money from Charlie. Have someone contact a driver or call a random taxi or known driver. Recruit locals to come with you so that you remain safe or are not taken advantage of by the taxi driver or vendor. Wait minutes or hours for the hired driver to arrive at Sunbeam to pick you up. Stop at multiple vendors, large and small, which may or may not be open at a particular time, regardless of the time of day. Determine if they have enough ice cream to serve sixty people, give or take ten or twenty. Assure you are not choosing an "adult" ice cream flavor in which savory flavors from beer, rum, or apple vodka are used, particularly and popularly, "Stout" ice cream, typically made with

Guinness or Dragon Stout. Shoot for Vanilla, Grape Nut, Coconut, Mango, Soursop or Guava. Haggle with vendor to convince them to accept U.S. Dollars. Make the calculation from Jamaican dollars to U.S. Dollars. Juggle one or two plastic-lined, seven-gallon cardboard boxes while sitting in the back seat of a taxi with two to five other people, attempting to keep the ice cream frozen in a hot, Caribbean climate, as you ride back to Sunbeam. In the one instance I am recalling, all fourteen gallons were consumed literally within moments, with caramel, chocolate, and strawberry syrup and peanuts as toppings, brought from Minnesota in our suitcases.

Nothing can be more ordinary for the typical American missionary such as myself than kitchen duty. I'm no kitchen superstar, believe me, but I did manage to provide nutrition enough to keep myself, one husband, and two children alive. I was fortunate that, even in our modest home, I had reliable appliances, modern conveniences, large prep surfaces, hot and cold water, and adequate wages to buy a cart full of groceries every so often.

I always took pleasure in spending large amounts of time in the kitchen at Sunbeam Children's Home in the early years, being the chief cook for most of our meals when we were there. In more recent years the hired cook, Mrs. Bryan, cooked many of our meals, but I always enjoyed my kitchen shifts, as I believe most of us did. I think it satisfied our parental and provider instincts to provide for our team and for the boys, and whatever the task, the more of us that were involved, the more fun and laughter spilled out from the kitchen. Additionally, kitchen duty was something we could do that produced tangible results, because when one is on a mission trip, tangible results are sometimes hard to come by.

The kitchen was, by far, the most shocking part of the Sunbeam building to new participants on the mission trips. In the early years, the roof leaked badly on that end of the building, particularly in the months after Hurricane Mitch in 1998. When it rained, the rainwater mixed with the garbage and dirt that seemed a permanent fixture on the floor, creating a muddy, slippery, filthy surface which then tracked to the rest of the building. A large, shallow tin for garbage sat under the concrete sink, always with a day or two worth of wet garbage. In the early years, the dogs, cats, and rodents wandered in and sniffed and took what they wanted and scurried away. Cockroaches and an assortment of other wildlife roamed the kitchen freely and we would brush them away as we cooked and as we ate.

When we first came to Sunbeam, each of us brought with us a plate, bowl, drinking cup and our silverware in a mesh bag, reminiscent of our old Boy or Girl Scout campouts. We washed our dishes in a three-stage process of cold water, cold bleach water, and cold rinse water, then hung our bags up to dry on a rope suspended over a long table in the dining room. The day's dishes for the boys, which could only be washed in cold water or water heated up on the stove, often sat until the next morning. There was only one dim light in the kitchen. Wooden louvered windows, open to the Jamaican breeze, were on one end and never did close completely.

Until about 2003, at which time we purchased a refrigerator that had a door that sealed shut and adequately cooled foods, we used a freezer for cooling. You see, the freezer did not do its freezing job, either. It had the capacity of cooling down to refrigerator temperature and not much cooler. So, into the freezer went such things as freshly purchased produce, perishables, the powdered milk we mixed up the night before. I made Jell-O one year in paper cups and held my breath as they set in the freezer. The refrigerator was not cold enough. The Jell-O was a success! One day I opened the refrigerator and there was a fully intact pig's head. Butcher day. I am not a farm girl. Set me back a few steps.

When we arrived in 2009, the chest freezer was taking its last gasps of life. The hinges had completely rusted out and the door, rather than being hinged on the back, simply sat atop the freezer without sealing. Charlie and Sherry went to Kingston to buy a new one with our team funds, and it was delivered the last afternoon we were at Sunbeam. As we opened the big box in excited anticipation, we were so discouraged to see numerous and significant dents covering the surface of the freezer. We had to leave for Minnesota the next day and knew we would not have the opportunity to personally follow through with communicating this to the vendor to receive a replacement. History had taught us that we could never be completely sure what would happen in this situation, and we were concerned that our hard-earned, thousand-dollar investment might be wasted when all the dust settled. We had no choice but to give instructions to Natalie, the Office Manager, depart on a plane back to Minnesota, and hope that everything would work out. And sure enough, Natalie did not let us down! We learned from an email later in the week that a new, dent-free freezer had been delivered and was working like a charm!

We generally ate cold cereal, toast, and *Tang* instant orange drink for breakfast, along with coffee. Cereal, powdered milk and a few megacans of *Tang* could easily be transported from Minnesota in our suitcases. One year we had to eat our breakfast in shifts, as the Sunbeam inventory was down to eight bowls.

A different year, we prepared toast on a large flat baking pan in the oven because the toaster had disappeared, and we boiled coffee on top of the gas stove, since the coffee pot had also disappeared. We were never sure what equipment and supplies we would find or not find in our Jamaican kitchen, even if they had been there the previous year, or even the previous week, or if we'd sent money to purchase it. Though these things sometimes still happen, disappearances of supplies and equipment are more a matter of wear and tear, and less about stealing or disappearing mysteriously. In the earlier years, things disappeared constantly. Kids would steal them and take them down the street to Gutter's Corner to sell or trade, use them as weapons, or just be careless and ruin them. Knives and other sharp objects would have to be locked up in the Director's office. The kitchen was the Wild West prior to Mrs. Bryan's arrival. Once there, she kept a close eye on utensils and equipment, and she demanded respect and appropriate behavior in the kitchen.

The boys' go-to dish for many meals is rice and peas, common throughout Jamaica. Want to eat like a Jamaican?

Jamaican Rice and Peas
1 cup canned red kidney beans (referred to as "peas" in Jamaica)
2 cups rice
1 cup coconut milk
4 cups water
2 tsp. thyme
2 green onions, chopped
½ c onion, chopped
Hot pepper flakes, to taste
Salt and pepper, to taste

Combine beans, water, coconut milk, thyme, green onions, and onions over medium heat until just boiling. Add salt, pepper, and hot pepper flakes to taste. Add rice, cover, and simmer over low heat for 25 minutes until rice is tender, and liquids have been absorbed. Check after 15 minutes and add more water if necessary. Serve warm.

One time, I needed to come up with one hundred cranberry orange muffins using only one twelve-muffin pan and one six-muffin pan. I baked one batch at a time, each batch taking double the sixteen-minute prescribed baking time. With each batch I got more creative, using tin cans and a variety of other receptacles as muffin tines. I decided that muffins can have a variety of appearances and it is of no consequence to forty growing boys and a bunch of hungry missionaries. Here's to cooking like a Jamaican!

Mrs. Bryan prudently respected the home's resources and tried her best to creatively feed the boys with whatever the meager pantry would provide. Whether she knew it or not, she followed the Jamaican proverb which stated, *"Willful was'e bring woeful wan'"* (Willful waste brings woeful want) (McLean 257). She delighted in making breakfast for the mission team each morning, which often consisted of some combination of eggs, callaloo (a spinach-like green), fried plantains, tea (Milo), fritters (basically, what we Minnesotans know as pancakes) and sometimes in the early years, akee and saltfish, the national dish of Jamaica.

To be polite, I initially gave the akee and saltfish a whirl, like most of us did, but I must admit that several of us had a little trouble loving it. This might be why Mrs. Bryan did not carry on the tradition of serving us this Jamaican delicacy. Apparently, it is an acquired taste. Ackee is the national fruit of Jamaica. Indigenous to the forests of the Ivory Coast and Gold Coast of West Africa, it was brought to Jamaica in 1793 by Captain Bligh to serve as food for the slave laborers. We saw many ackee trees as we drove across the country.

The akee fruit has two large, dark, grape-like blobs on it that are poisonous and thus, not edible. The akee must be allowed to open fully or at least partly before it is detached from the tree. The yellow, fleshy arils around the big seeds are often boiled in salt water or milk, then lightly fried in butter. In Jamaica, it is often cooked with salted codfish, onions, and tomatoes to make akee and saltfish. Another option is to add the akee to a stew of beef, salt-pork, scallions, thyme, and other seasonings, or simply curry it and serve over rice. In Mrs. Bryan's case, akee and saltfish was the preparation method of choice.

Though I would always discretely place some cold cereal and milk out on the table when akee and saltfish was served, we were usually able to fool one of the new people into taking a big forkful of it. Case in point, 2003, when Pastor Corey said enthusiastically to Al, the new guy, "This stuff is really good! Try it!" Al placed a huge forkful of akee and saltfish into his mouth and looked as if he would upchuck. Todd appeared to be the only one who could handle it that year. Some adventurous eaters have, over the years, acquired a taste for the national dish, but I am unable to recall any of them, and certainly was not one of them myself.

Our kitchen cooking adventures were many. Grilled cheese sandwiches were a staple for several years, and we became quite adept, over time, at slicing a melted hunk of Velveeta cheese product into portions that could be slapped between two slices of bread and put on one of three-or-so griddles we had heated up for the purpose of serving sixty-plus people. We sometimes brought one griddle of our own, never knowing from year to year if the griddles we brought the previous year would still be there. A packaged rice with canned chicken thrown in became a quick Minnesota hotdish that tasted might good after a long day of work. Canned vegetables are easy to transport from Minnesota, we have had our share of canned corn and canned green beans. *Pringle's* potato chips are a staple. We generally bring up to twenty-five cans of Pringles with us on any given trip to Jamaica.

Though we have local fruit available, we sometimes bring canned fruit with us to assure that we do indeed have fruit to eat. We were never sure what fresh fruits we could pick up at the markets, roadside stands, or from the fruit trees in the backyard or at the neighbor's house. We always provide evening snacks, something the boys do not normally receive unless a visiting mission team is present. *Rice Krispie* bars, popcorn, *Oreo* cookies, granola, and brownies were all hits with the kids.

Each year spaghetti is on the menu, again because it is easy to transport from Minnesota. It has taken many years, as westernized tastes have slowly made their way into the Jamaican palate, for the boys' taste buds and stomachs to adjust to American spaghetti sauce. Initially, they were not interested in the spaghetti sauce and would instead have noodles with butter. We take the wonderful Jamaican hard bread that is delivered to Sunbeam several times a week, slather it with butter, sprinkle with garlic salt, and place it on the griddle briefly: garlic toast for our spaghetti! Sliced, fresh bananas from the backyard add a little nutrition to the giant can of chocolate pudding that came in a suitcase. We have made tuna sandwiches—did you know that Miracle Whip survives, unrefrigerated in a hot Jamaican kitchen?—and scalloped potatoes and ham, and other typical American fare. Mrs. Bryan often uses fresh vegetables to create salads for us. Cabbage and lettuce are prone to creating "running belly," so it must be washed, the first few layers taken off, and soaked in salt water for a while. My own experience with "running belly" due to cabbage made my 2018 trip to Sunbeam way more interesting than I would have chosen.

On one occasion in the early years, I made cherry cheesecake and put it in the freezer, hoping the freezer was cold enough for the cheesecake to set. It worked, and my team thought I was a gourmet cook. Fajitas were a hit one evening. I was told it was a four-star meal. When one has been working all day, hasn't really slept well for a while, is slightly incoherent, and compliments the cook on her cooking, the cook can take the compliment and get a big head, or she can step back and realize that she could have given them deep fried goat and they would eat it and love it and give it a decent compliment. In the early days, hot dogs were usually on the menu once or twice per week, as they could be purchased at the store on Gutter's Corner. However, it's a little frightening to ponder what might be in a Jamaican hot dog. They are generally not on the menu anymore.

One year recently, I had what I thought was a brilliant idea to make rolled out sugar cookies (known to many Minnesotans as "cut-outs") in various shapes and have the boys help decorate them with various colors of powdered sugar frosting and other decorations, something I love to do with my own grandchildren. I packed in my suitcases all the supplies and groceries I needed for the project, except for the flour, which Sunbeam had in bulk in the pantry. I looked through my large collection of cookie cutters at home and found shapes that my Jamaica boys might find familiar: chickens, dolphins, pigs, flowers, trees, stars, circles. I collected all the ingredients and supplies that had come to Jamaica in our team luggage: cookie cutters, rolling pin, food coloring, powdered sugar, and more.

It was all going well as I gathered a few volunteers to work on mixing up the dough and baking the cookies. What I did not count on was the condition of the flour, not an optional ingredient. When I opened the big barrel of bulk flour in the Sunbeam pantry, I discovered that it was full of flour weevils, little light brown, six-legged worm-like creatures that love to make their homes in grains and flourish in warm, humid conditions like Jamaican pantries. Having added all the ingredients together except the flour and having planned and spent a large amount of time preparing for the sugar cookies, Pastor Shannon suggested we have a weevil-picking party and proceed with the cookies! After an hour or so of several of us picking out the weevils, we called the cookie dough good to go, deciding that semi-spotted sugar cookies would suffice, and the oven would probably kill any detrimental effects of the weevils.

Another slight roadblock was the lack of consideration of the 100-plus degree temperature in the kitchen. The dough was so sticky that it did not cut into the delightful shapes we had planned; instead, we settled for mystery blobs. But in the end, we had a pile of a few hundred cookies of various unidentifiable shapes, and the boys enjoyed frosting, decorating, and then devouring their own cookies in about two minutes flat. The boys thought they were the best thing they had ever eaten. Despite my initial excitement about this project, I decided that we would just chalk that one up to experience and perhaps move on to other treats in the future.

Typically, we had eaten separate from the boys for the evening meal. We fed them first at their normal place in the dining room, then cleared them out, got organized, and fed ourselves in the same dining room afterward. About five years ago, our team began the tradition of serving a big family-style meal to our team and the boys together once each week we were there: meat gravy over homemade biscuits, mashed potatoes, corn, and dessert, or some variation of this meal. Serving family style, i.e., large serving bowls of food in the middle of the table, passed around from one person to the next, was initially somewhat of a risk for this crowd. The boys were accustomed to being handed a plateful of food, with generous portions, but never enough for a growing boy, especially for many of whom did not eat adequate meals prior to coming to Sunbeam and tended to hoard food. But as the years went by and the boys grew accustomed to a more disciplined and food secure environment, we decided to give it a try.

Instructions were given to the boys beforehand about taking reasonable portions so that everyone would have enough to eat. We mentioned to them many times that, if the boys who served themselves first took too much, the boys at the end of the table would have nothing to eat. And much credit should be given to Superintendent Whitley for preparing the boys for this event. We wanted so badly for it to work.

The first time we tried serving family style, it was a smashing success. We set up tables and benches in the large central living area of the home. We invited all the staff to eat with us and, in later years, had the staff invite their own families to join us. It became an event that all looked forward to each time our team visited Sunbeam. We said a table prayer together and spread ourselves out among the boys to eat our meal. We ate as a family because we felt like a family.

In this new experiment, the boys were respectful and kind. They seemed proud to share with each other, as well as to follow directions and earn praise from Mr. Whitley and from us. We made huge quantities of food for this meal, and in most cases, could give seconds and even sometimes had food left at the end. And we heard comments from the boys like, "Thank you, Miss Mary," "Thank you, Miss Cindy," and best of all, "My stomach is full." I wondered how many times these boys would have had an occasion in their lives to say that their stomachs were full. This tradition has continued since that time, with mostly positive results, though its success can easily be derailed based on the number of boys and the extent of their previous food insecurity.

On day in 2003, Mrs. Bryan informed me that there was not enough chicken to feed us all for supper and asked if I would walk to Gutter's Corner and use the team money to buy it. I asked a few of the boys to accompany me for safety reasons and set out on foot for Gutter's Corner in search of chicken. Seems simple enough, right? But I had not purchased fresh chicken in Jamaica previously. I walked to one of the two food stores on Gutter's Corner and told them I needed chicken. I had no idea how it was sold and in what quantities. For all I knew, they would go out back and hand me a clucking chicken.

The storekeeper asked me how much chicken I needed, to which I replied, "Um…how do you sell it?" I ended up, when all was said and done, with two seven-pound hunks of frozen chicken parts. I could not identify, in their frozen state, just what parts these were, and I really do not care to know. But I returned to Sunbeam victorious, with fourteen pounds of something at least resembling chicken, as well as soft drinks for my shopping companions and enough bread for one more meal. Alas, another successful Jamaican shopping mission. That evening, Mrs. Bryan prepared fried chicken, mashed potatoes, fresh tomatoes, cucumbers, and lettuce for us. She generally completes meals by 2:30 in the afternoon, to be eaten at 5:30. The food sits out on plates for those three hours. We ate it, it was delicious, and the team survived another day, as far as I know, without running belly.

Shopping in Jamaica has changed somewhat in the years we have been travelling to Jamaica, with more modern stores all the time. However, there are still many stores that have sold their wares the same way for decades. The storekeeper and merchandise are separated from the shopper by bars or heavy chain link fencing from counter height to the ceiling. This is done for the security of the merchandise and safety of the shopkeeper due to the prevalence of theft. From groceries to nails to chicken feed, this is how we shop at the Gutter's Corner shops and in most small towns.

Macaroni and cheese was often supplemented with cut-up hot dogs in the early days. One time, I over-shot on the macaroni a bit. A lot, in fact. Even thirty-five hungry boys and fifteen team members eating seconds and thirds could not eat what I had prepared. So, out of sight of the boys and the staff so I wouldn't appear wasteful, I gave the pigs a feast of macaroni and cheese. These pigs were the skinniest pigs I had ever seen. When the pigs saw someone coming toward the pigpen with something they thought might be edible, some of the bigger pigs stood up on their hind legs with front legs on the pen door like a dog, to await the feast with a look of anticipation. As I walked through the muck surrounding the pigpen, which suctioned around my ankles with each succeeding step, I presented the excited pigs with this feast by dumping large mounds of macaroni and cheese into the two pigpens. These were happy, happy pigs, if only temporarily before the running belly probably kicked in.

On that hog-feeding mission, I returned in a dirty, sweaty, smelly state to the kitchen where I helped Mrs. Bryan prepare what she believed to be an American supper of hamburgers and French fries, both of which were deep-fried. The hamburgers, as most Jamaican food Mrs. Bryan prepared, were spicy, covered with a tangy sauce that had an unidentifiable Jamaican flavor. The boys do get a variety of food that is not nearly as bland as it was before she arrived on the scene. Deep frying is the easiest because oil is plentiful, and the frying can be done in a heavy pot of oil right on the stovetop. Baking in the oven creates excess heat and takes considerably longer than average because of its inefficiency.

As I look back on the early Sunbeam visits, it seems as though the menus we came up with seem so simple, but nothing is simple, by American standards, in the Sunbeam kitchen. One was never sure if the water would be in service, though that became less and less of a problem as the years went by and a new water collection and filtration system was installed. And because the oven door did not close completely, it took a higher temperature and about twice as long to bake anything. Because of the lack of appropriate pans, baking dishes, muffin tins or other utensils, large quantities sometimes needed to be done in many smaller quantities. Then there was the issue of keeping those finished portions clear of the ever-present ants, bugs, and cockroaches in the kitchen, not to mention the hovering, hungry boys. And, of course, with unreliable refrigeration, food often sat out in nearly three-digit temperatures for long periods of time before being eaten.

We knew we, as visitors, were not accustomed to eating in such conditions and probably had two options: (1) everything would taste great, process correctly or mostly correctly in our bodies, and we would come through just fine or with only minor discomforts; or (2) things wouldn't go so well, and we'd get "running belly." Our eating philosophy early on was to bring our own food, as well as to cook it both for ourselves and for the boys, in order to avoid the types of germs, parasites, and other nasties that come with eating in a third world environment out of a kitchen teeming with many forms of wildlife. The first few years, it was even suggested we take preventative does of both antibiotics and stomach relief meds, just in case.

Over the years, as the condition of the home and the kitchen improved, stainless steel countertops were installed, and Mrs. Bryan was hired and used more sanitary techniques in the kitchen, we gradually became more comfortable and adventurous eating Mrs. Bryan's wonderful meals which she took great pride in preparing for us. At different times in our history there, she prepared either the noon or the evening meal for us and we prepared our own breakfast and one of the other meals, both for us and for the staff and boys. However, I have no doubt that, having learned our wimpy Minnesota tastes over the years, Mrs. Bryan has learned to tame down the dishes considerably from her normal recipes. We have come to greatly appreciate Jamaican food, often well-seasoned with allspice (in Jamaica, known as pimento), peppers or pepper flakes, and lots of curry flavor. Curry is a combination of many spices such as turmeric, cardamom, cumin, cinnamon, mace, and others. Ginger is also commonly used in Jamaican cooking, as well as for other purposes such as calming stomachs on those cross-island trips with ginger beer or ginger candy. Curry chicken, curry goat, jerk chicken, oxtail, snapper, ackee and saltfish, with side dishes of bammy, festival, fried dumplings, callaloo, fried plantains, and boiled green bananas: we've eaten it all, with various degrees of satisfaction depending on who one asks. My personal favorite meal from Mrs. Bryan? Coconut chicken and pineapple shish kabobs. Oh my, it is good.

Mrs. Bryan is a master at scheduling and preparing meals for the boys on staggered school schedules, but she handles it like a champ.

Some of the boys go to school at seven o'clock in the morning and are back around noon. Others depart Sunbeam late in the morning and are home by late afternoon. Still others leave in the mid-afternoon and do not get back until mid-evening. As onlookers, just when we thought every boy was fed, another few came wandering into the kitchen looking for their meals. Mrs. Bryan always seemed to know exactly how many meals she needed to have plated and sitting out on the counter for every last boy that came home from school.

I wrote in my 2003 journal about my first encounter with Mrs. Bryan, whom I have come to dearly love. Over the years, we have always greeted each other with the biggest, best hug. She is thin, with a face that is either sporting a big smile or a deep sense of purpose. She lives on Gutters Corner, a few blocks down the road, and arrives at Sunbeam at five o'clock in the morning to immediately begin preparing breakfast for the boys, as well as lunch, on the weekdays. Her shift ends at around two o'clock in the afternoon. A weekend cook takes over to give her a break on Saturdays and Sundays. The evening meal is served by other staff members except when teams are present, at which time the visiting team takes over and prepares and serves the evening meal to the boys and staff members who are still there at that time of day.

Mrs. Bryan generally wears a denim skirt, a t-shirt, and a full-coverage apron. I greet her every day with, "Good morning, my darling" in the best Patois accent I can summon. That is how Miss Nora, the house mother in 1995, greeted each one of us each morning. Mrs. Bryan laughs at my feeble attempt at the Patois dialect and gives me a big hug. What a wonderful thing to be told, "Miss Heidi, you put a smile on my face." I spend a lot of time in the kitchen with Mrs. Bryan, as do many of us, and feel a special connection with her. I am quite sure that having a team around isn't a bed of roses when you are already cooking for 50 people or thereabouts. Our teams do alleviate some of the pressure in the kitchen by cooking the evening meal, but we also create more pressure by adding up to 20 more people for breakfast and any other meals she specially prepares for us. Mrs. Bryan takes it all in stride and serves as a mother figure to us, to the boys, and an inspiration to many of us.

The Sunbeam pantry is an essential part of its operation. Feeding thirty to forty growing boys is a tall order and incredibly expensive for Sunbeam. The boys now eat relatively healthily compared to the past, but it does depend on the level of food stock in the pantry. We are constantly amazed at Mrs. Bryan's ability to "make something out of nothing" and stretch a tin of mackerel fifty ways. It is like the stories many of us remember hearing from our Depression era parents or grandparents who had to make do with the meager provisions they had, relying on their garden, Mama's resourcefulness, and sometimes only the grace of God.

Looking around the pantry at Sunbeam, one might find these things: Mackerel fillets in tomato sauce, sardines in hot sauce, Vienna sausage, canned chicken, *Foska* oats, *Milo*, cream crackers, black beans, rice, bread, and oil. When we travel to Sunbeam, especially in the last several years, one of our goals is always to raise enough money to fill the pantry. Much of the food we bring to fill the pantry comes in our suitcases. We, along with the boys, do eat much of that food over the time we are there. So, a few of the team members often accompany Mrs. Bryan on a food shopping expedition near the end of our stay to purchase enough food to fill the pantry once again. Our goal is always to leave a full pantry when we depart.

Though our gifts of food do not last long with so many mouths to feed, at least it supplies the basics for a while. Sunbeam receives occasional quantities of rice from Food for the Poor, but otherwise relies on their own resources to provide food for the boys. It is a constant challenge to feed the boys three meals a day with so few resources. So, we do the best we can, and know that the boys eat better than a lot of Jamaican children. The neighborhood children have been known to say in recent years, "I wish I could live there."

A common staple at Sunbeam is breadfruit, brought to Jamaica in the late 1700s as food for the slave laborers on the sugar plantations. I have learned, and the number could be inexact due to the passing of such information through oral history, that about three hundred breadfruit trees arrived on a ship in Jamaica in that timeframe and were distributed throughout the island. Breadfruit is a nutritious melon. It has the starchy consistency of unripe potatoes and as it ripens, it softens to about the consistency of a mango, but without the mango's sweetness. And breadfruit grows on the Sunbeam property.

Mrs. Bryan uses breadfruit as a staple in the boys' diet, as it is plentiful and filling. When needed for an upcoming meal, I observed "Cowboy", the resident farmer at the time, build a small wood fire and throw several recently picked breadfruit directly into the fire. There they stayed for approximately thirty minutes. They were then peeled, cut up, and fried in oil. Though breadfruit is considered a fruit, fried breadfruit tastes, to our American tongues, like fried potatoes, requiring salt and Ketchup for some of us Minnesota weirdos, whereas the locals eat it as is, often for breakfast.

Nothing is more ordinary than water. Or so we Americans think. In our early visits to Sunbeam, disruptions in the water supply were more frequent than we would normally be comfortable with. One morning in 1998, typical of other mornings during those years, we woke up to a situation in which there was no water supply. It quit at some point during the night, so no showers, no toilets, no drinks. We had been introduced early on to the trick of keeping a water supply in buckets in case they were needed for flushing, but true to Murphy's Law, had not done so the prior night. Water service returned by around 6:30 that evening, so things were a bit stinky that day, but in typical Jamaican fashion, our attitude had to be, "No problem, Mon."

Late afternoon showers work well for most of us, as we are usually so hot, sweaty, and exhausted by then that a shower is much needed and welcomed. There are two toilets and two shower stalls in each dorm. While there have been many improvements in both the structure and infrastructure of the home, the showers have not changed. They consist of concrete block stalls about three feet wide, with a rod and a plastic shower curtain. Cold water comes out of a water pipe in the wall, without a shower head, with little or no water pressure. The water sort of falls out of the wall. It sometimes gets down to a slow trickle and, in the early years, often came to a complete halt. That didn't happen once the new water storage facility and filtration system was installed. I still warn the troops, however, to never put on more soap or shampoo than they are willing to wipe off with a towel.

The miraculous thing that happens is that, by the end of our time at Sunbeam, a cold shower seems very normal and practical. If there's a little soap and some shampoo involved, it's a very efficient way to get clean, and gives us a little kick to get us through the dinner hour and evening activities until we can crash.

On the topic of "ordinary things," nothing is more ordinary for boys than playing outside. The Sunbeam boys don't sit around in the house. If they are not eating, sleeping, or doing their chores or homework, they are outside just being boys. Visiting teams have built a basketball court in the backyard, and football (what we North Americans know as soccer) games are constant. Competitive marble playing is a regular activity. With picnic tables scattered around in the shade of the building, we always bring along games, crafts, and projects to spread out on those tables to engage the boys. On one rainy Sunday afternoon after church, we divided the boys into six groups of three or four and set up six game stations. The boys rotated every fifteen minutes throughout the afternoon to the various stations. The stations were the same activities that many of us baby boomers enjoyed as kids: hacky sack, football toss, jacks, Twister, card tricks; and Jenga. The boys loved it, and we enjoyed yet another way to develop relationships that lead to meaningful conversation, creative expression, learning, and fun. One year we brought hundreds of small balloons with us in our suitcases. On a Sunday afternoon, we filled them with water, got the team and the boys together in the backyard, and had a friendly water balloon fight.

In 2009, a local Jamaican service club had recently donated new mattresses for the boys' beds. This meant the old mattresses were pulled out and stacked outside the back door to be burned. But until that happened, these mattresses provided an opportunity for the boys to run at top speed down the back hallway, turn a corner, and launch from the concrete steps onto a high stack of mattresses. In my mother mode, I envisioned a young boy rebounding from the mattresses onto the adjacent concrete, but as in so many other cases, I just had to enjoy the fact that they were having a great time, and that these boys were tough, not America tough but Jamaica tough. They then dragged the mattresses, one by one, out to the middle of the backyard and turned them into gymnastics mats, where flips and handsprings and acrobatics were performed. They ran and jumped at full speed until dinnertime and could hardly stay awake during our evening program. That's the sign of a good, good day for a boy, in Jamaica or anywhere.

One year, team member Scott brought loads of Matchbox cars that he had painted white, along with dozens of multi-colored Sharpie markers. The boys spent hours designing and painting their sportscars and then proudly asking for someone to take a picture of them with their cars. Each year we bring out the favorite games, as well as teach them new board games and card games. We have made wooden cross necklaces that they proudly sported the entire time we were there. We play games that have been standards in our own childhoods or with our own children: jacks, Play-Doh, Checkers, Chess, Twister. There is always action on those picnic tables, just doing normal things that children like to do.

My short-term mission experiences in Jamaica and the work on my master's degree thesis on Jamaican folklorist Louise Bennett converge in the area of "ordinary things." One of the reasons I chose to write about Louis Bennett in my thesis was that she wrote about those ordinary things and not only that, but she chose to write in the language of the common people of Jamaica rather than in the Standard English of the British colonists. As a child educated in colonized Jamaica, she was indoctrinated with the language and images from a country and culture that was not her own: England. As a result, when she first started to write poems, it was in Standard English.

However, an incident on an electric tram car in Jamaica's capitol city of Kingston when Miss Lou was a teenager resulted in the writing of her first verse in Jamaican Patois. Bennett found the language to be vital and expressive of the daily life of her Jamaican experience: the "normal" things. She never returned to Standard English as a medium in which to express herself, either in her written work or her oral performances.

On those electric tram cars, the primary means of public transportation in Kingston, people with baskets were required to sit in back. The trams were typically overflowing with people and the people who sat in the back were often reluctant to squeeze together to allow someone else to sit next to them, especially someone of the lower class, or a "one-dress woman," as Bennett refers to her. So, the speaker in this poem tells her fellow riders to spread themselves out to take more room so that the poor, common woman will not fit. As Louis Bennett boarded the tram car, she overheard one of the women in the back of the bus say, "Pread out yuhself, one dress-oman come." Bennett's resulting verse is written in the language of the common people of Jamaica, commonly referred to as Jamaican "Patois" (pat-WAH), Jamaican Creole, or Jamaican Dialect. The verse began this way:

> "Pread out yuhself deh Liza, one
> Dress-oman dah look like sey
> She see di li space side-a we
> An waan foce herself een deh."
> (Bennett, "On a Tramcar," quoted in Morris, Selected Poems v)

Bennett had found her literary language, by expressing the views of the masses, in the language of the masses, about the daily lives of the masses.

Jamaican Patois had its roots in the African slaves that were brought to work in Jamaica's sugar plantations in the seventeenth century and beyond. The enslaved workers struggled to make their home in the Caribbean by molding, from the Standard English used in England, a language that reflected their African roots. Slaves were forced to use Standard English when they interacted with the masters and later, to interact in a society in which it was the language of the colonial institutions, such as the educational system. But among themselves, they spoke in a language that reflected the reality of their own history, tradition, and experience. It drew most of its vocabulary from English, but also a significant amount of grammar and vocabulary from various African languages, some Spanish influence from the period in which Jamaica was a territory of Spain, some Arawak influence from the few vestiges of Arawak culture left with its remaining slaves, and later, influences from other groups that were brought in as plantation workers. This poem by Guyanan Grace Nichols refers to the creation of Jamaican Patois:

"I have crossed an ocean,
I have lost my tongue.
From the root of the old one
A new one has sprung."
(from "Epilogue" by Grace Nichols, quoted in Thompson, 45)

Jamaican Patois emerged through Jamaica's history as the speech of the lower class, a language that was considered a corruption of Standard English. The continuing imposition of Standard English and a lack of recognition of Jamaican Patois served as a means of oppressing the subordinate cultural group in colonial Jamaica, long after slavery was abolished, and until Jamaican Independence in 1962 and beyond.

In modern Jamaica, Patois has continued its evolution and is widely spoken among most socioeconomic groups. As such, nearly all the children at Sunbeam Children's Home, though able to understand and speak in American English, delight in breaking into their more comfortable and familiar Patois with little grins on their faces, knowing we Americans have steep learning curves in understanding what the boys are talking about. All of the short-term mission groups that have landed at Sunbeam have experienced the beautiful lull of Jamaican Patois as the boys chatter back and forth, and some of us have delighted in having the boys teach us some of the common Patois vocabulary and phrases, which they do as they laugh hysterically at our attempts to mimic it. Following are a few expressions I have learned over the years, but unfortunately sound hopelessly Minnesotan in my execution.

- I'll be right back: *Mi soon come*
- Well done: *Big up, Respect*
- See you later: *Walk good*
- What's up? What's going on?: *Wah gwaan?*
- Everything is good: *Mi deh yah, Evryting criss*
- Relax/chill: *Easy nuh*
- Have a nice day: *Bless up*
- Where are you?: *Weh yuh deh?*
- This is how we do it: *A suh wi dweets*
- I'll be there soon: *Soon forward*
- Misbehave: *Bruck out*
- Singing, dancing, having a good time: *Jammin*

Whether it's cooking, laundry, playing with the boys, working around the home, shopping for daily provisions, or trying to decipher the boys' use of Patois, it's the "ordinary-ness" of those things that makes our immersive mission experience so valuable in truly understanding and celebrating the Jamaican culture, thus having a bigger impact both on the boys' lives and ours.

Chapter 7

Lesson: Find Joy

We must make a deliberate choice to choose joy. Happiness is related to our external selves, things like having enough money to pay the mortgage and put food on the table, having enough money to pay the cable bill and feed our family, having meaningful relationships with friends and our significant other. Happiness is based on circumstances. Joy is at a deeper level: a "It is well-with-my-soul" level, as I once read. First, we choose joy, and then we are called to share that joy.

Sharing this joy is what God intends in short-term mission work. But the nature and purpose of short-term missions is also a place where diverging views occur. Some believe that short-term missions must take the form of swooping in to impose our ways—our will—to "convert the natives." I think of it differently. I believe that we simply go in as faithful servants and work through their already-established daily lives, cultures, and systems, and live among them to build trustful, joyful, and respectful relationships. We then allow God to do the work through us, however that may occur. It's a bit more of a measured, low-key approach to missions. One meets the boys where they are, as opposed to beating them over the head with a frying plan. Agree or disagree, it is how I have personally approached my short-term mission experiences, and how I use it as a means of spreading joy that comes with a relationship with our Creator.

It is our job as missionaries to share the joy. Kevin is one Sunbeam resident who knows how to share the joy right back. He has autism, epilepsy, and is legally blind. Kevin is filled with joy and spreads it to others without even trying. Whereas the other boys move on to a transition program and leave Sunbeam at around age eighteen, Kevin has been allowed to stay throughout the years, serving somewhat as a goodwill ambassador for Sunbeam. He would be unable to live independently and has no family active in his life. His family members are the staff members and his Sunbeam brothers. He will always be Mr. Sunbeam. Very few things are the same as they were when our group first visited Sunbeam in 1995, but for those of us who have been traveling there for many, many years, Kevin is one of the constants. He is part of the familiarity and comfort that we return to each time we visit.

Much of Kevin's day is spent sitting in the common area or on a bench in the backyard, engaged in his familiar rocking motion, taking in the sounds around him, and often talking or singing to no one in particular, always with a smile on his face. His ability to see shadows and to extinguish between light and darkness allow him to know when someone walks by, and Kevin sees this as an opportunity to call out a name, any name that is familiar to him, to start a conversation. A few days into each team's visit, Kevin has already developed the ability to recognize individual voices and can often discern who might be walking by. Each time I walk up to him or walk past him, I call out his name, Kevin!", and he responds with "Miss Eidi!" and then, "Are we having biscuits for supper?"

There are four things that dominate Kevin's daily life: (1) Eating, (2) Music, (3) Jesus, and (4) making sure his shirt is tucked in. I am not sure of the priority order of those four things, but all are very important in his life. And anyone who stops for a conversation with Kevin generally ends up talking about one of those four things. He loves to sing, has memorized about every song he ever heard, and enjoys food more than anybody I know. "Miss Eidi! Is it lunchtime?" he asks regularly, regardless of the time of day. He loves going to church and can be heard singing loudly and listening intently. He's a simple guy; he's a happy guy; he brings joy to so many.

It is a beautiful thing to see the young boys take care of Kevin. While Kevin has unfortunately been the subject of teasing at times from the new boys when they first come to Sunbeam, the boys seem to come to an understanding rather quickly that they need to take special care and look out for him. Each year we visit, it seems that one or two of the younger boys has developed a closer relationship with Kevin and takes on the role of looking after him. I will never lose the image in my mind of one of the young boys dragging an unconscious Kevin by his outstretched arms across the yard, toward the home, after Kevin had a seizure while outside in the backyard. He wanted to get Kevin to a place of safety and did it the only way he knew how.

Inevitably, when it is time to eat, one of the boys will lead Kevin to the dining room, though Kevin's nose leads him there just fine if no one is around to help. He licks his plate clean and will always accept second and third portions if given the opportunity. He proceeds to talk about his meal and previous meals if one is interested in listening. Plain and simple, I love Kevin, and he has taught me that you can find joy in even the simplest things. Like eating biscuits and making sure your shirt is tucked in.

An important part of our mission experience is to plan and carry out evening programming, usually revolving around a weekly theme. It is a joyful time, led by a pastor or church staff member and musicians that have come with our group. We always involve the boys in the fun. The get-together always involves singing, a few words from the pastor, and perhaps skits with the boys as the key actors. And most of all it usually involves loud, raucous fun. Depending on the composition of the team, there may be guitars, keyboards, handmade drums or maracas, and singing voices of all levels and competencies. If our team does not include a pastor, we fill in as needed. There are elements of Sunday School, Vacation Bible School, summer camp, and *America's Got Talent*, all rolled into one thirty- to forty-five-minute session. We sing, clap, dance, laugh, pray, and have an evening snack.

One year our team brought kazoos and fake Halloween teeth that provided many moments of laughter, both from curious onlookers at the airport and from the Sunbeam boys. Another year we put a few benches end to end, sat our entire team on them, one leg on each side of the bench, and pretended we were the Jamaican Bobsled Team as we sang a ridiculous song of some sort. One evening in 2009, the boys wanted to teach us "whiteys" how to dance to reggae music. Twins Neil and Oneil gave us a dancing demo, and we were off, bouncing, twisting, and moving in mysterious ways, truly having fun and letting loose, despite being the subjects of uproarious laughter from our Jamaica boys. It was all going well until Charlie sprained his knee. Our conclusion: We Scandinavian Lutherans should probably stick with bobbing our heads inconspicuously to the music as we lightly and rhythmically tap one hand on a leg.

One evening, we traded national anthems. The boys stood respectfully and proudly as they loudly sang the Jamaican national anthem, a prayer for a land that is so loved by its people, despite the nation's struggles:

> *Eternal Father, bless our land,*
> *Guard us with Thy mighty hand.*
> *Keep us free from evil powers,*
> *Be our light through countless hours.*
> *To our leaders, Great Defender,*
> *Grant true wisdom from above.*
> *Justice, truth, be ours forever,*
> *Jamaica, land we love.*
> *Jamaica, Jamaica, Jamaica, land we love.*

Teach us true respect for all,
Stir response to duty's call.
Strengthen us the weak to cherish,
Give us vision lest we perish.
Knowledge send us, Heavenly Father,
Grant true wisdom from above

Then, with our hands on our hearts, we Minnesotans all sang our own national anthem. It was, interestingly, a very emotional experience. After that day, I became much more of a heart-holding, lump-in-the-throat national anthem singer. I remember coming back home to Minnesota that year and attending a high school basketball game in our little town, a common occurrence for me and for my family. With my hand over my heart and tears welling up in my eyes, I was taken aback by the emotions that I felt when the national anthem was played, and I have felt this way every single time since.

I think back on Pastors Duane, Kathy, Corey, Keith, Shannon and others, and the gifts they brought to Sunbeam with their ability to relate to the kids, their musical talent in many cases, and the right words to make our theme come alive to the boys. And the lay music leaders such as Bill, Becky, Dwight, Brooke, Barb, Matt, and others. What a blessing these nightly get-togethers were, not only for the boys but for us, spread amongst the kids on the benches in the living room, worshipping together in our own unique way. And Kevin? This was his favorite part of the day, except for meals, of course. He sang along with each song, clapped, and capped it all off with a nighttime snack. Kevin, especially, was living large during those evening programs, sharing the joy.

Sometimes we had devotions at five o'clock in the morning, a much more low-key but no less impactful and joyful gathering of the team and the boys. One such early morning session in 2014 stands out, when Pastor Keith accompanied the team to Sunbeam. He had written a small prayer, a blessing of sorts, which the boys were asked to pair up and read to their partners during that morning session. The boys were each given a handwritten copy of the blessing, and though initially shy about it, looked their partner in the eye and read it to him, on the last day we were all together before the team departed. Here is the blessing:

When I see you,
I see me.
God lives where you live,
And goes wherever you go.
God loves you
God bless you

As it turned out, it was meaningful for the boys, and many of them remembered it. When we left Sunbeam that year, one of the boys held his hand up to the bus window from the outside, where Pastor Keith was sitting inside. Keith put his hand to the window in the same place, from the inside, palm to palm with the boy. The boy said to Keith, "When I see you, I see me."

Bill, a former music teacher and then-Minister of Music at our church, was a true blessing to have with us on the team now and then. His musical talent and kind spirit were such joys to witness as he interacted with the boys and with us. One year when both Bill and another local musician, Barb, joined us on the team, our music game was strong. We had brought along two guitars to be donated to Sunbeam. Barb taught any interested boy how to play, and there was rarely a moment that week when we did not hear a guitar strumming somewhere off in the distance. The boys were eager guitar students, and the guitars took a beating. I have a sweet photo of Sunbeam boy Jermain serenading his special friend, my then-teenage daughter, Sara, with the guitar. At one of the evening programs near the end of the week, Barb tenderly assisted Omar, newly proficient in a total of three guitar chords, through a song especially chosen to use just those three chords. During that same week, Bill gave voice lessons to Feial, Joel, and Ricardo. The nature of our evening programming was often dependent upon the talents of the team members who were there that year. The joy spread through music, the universal language, was contagious.

One day when visiting Strathmore Children's Home in 1995, I met LaToya, whom we learned was 16 years old. From what we would learn, she had been dropped off at Strathmore at some point in the recent past. She had not gotten along with her mother, so had been sent to live with her grandmother. But her grandmother, with other extended family members living in her modest home, discovered that she could not afford to have another mouth to feed in the household. So, LaToya had been dropped off at Strathmore, and was told, "Someone will come and pick you up tomorrow." According to the house mother at Strathmore, LaToya spent most of her days sitting alone in a hard-backed wooden chair in the entryway to the home, facing the street, waiting. LaToya did not even know who she was waiting for, but she was waiting. That person never came.

One of our team members who was visiting with me that day was a social worker by profession, and spent much of the day with LaToya, eventually getting her to open up a bit, and even make her smile. LaToya's eyes sparkled and she became animated when she talked about her dream of becoming a beautician. It gave her such joy to talk about it. We wanted that joy to become a reality, even if it was just in a small way. Team member Patsy asked LaToya if she would be willing to do her—Patsy's—hair in Jamaican braids. LaToya did so with great joy and pride, and Patsy sported some beautifully braided locks for the remainder of our time in Jamaica. LaToya felt valued, at least for one small portion of one day in her life, and that joy in doing something she loved was a brief respite from her life circumstances. Sometimes we missionaries can provide only small gifts, but they are still gifts, and I am happy for the pure joy that LaToya felt on that day.

It is important to note that the conditions have changed at Strathmore Children's since many of these things occurred. It is now known as "Strathmore Gardens Children's Home." Sometime after our initial visits to Strathmore in the mid and late 1990s, a pastor from Chicago took over the home and ran it for a period of time. Currently it is licensed by the Government of Jamaica under the Child Development Agency, so is a government entity. It houses children aged thirteen and under, serving as a safe space for children to stay while family matters are being resolved, with the ultimate objective being to reunite children with their families.

In the time that has elapsed since many of the disturbing things I witnessed there, I have seen and heard stories of Jamaica Broilers (the local chicken factory) and the Supreme Ventures Foundation (SVF) conducting service projects at Strathmore such as updating fire and emergency systems; painting and repairing walls and play structures; and other safety and beautification projects. This stemmed from multiple tragic incidents, mainly fires, at children's homes in recent years, as well as audits done since those events revealing gaps in fire safety infrastructure. Fire safety equipment such as smoke detectors and fire extinguishers, signage, evacuation maps, fire safety education and training for the staff have all occurred at Strathmore, something that would have seemed unimaginable in the early years when we visited.

In a discussion about joy, few people express as much joy as does Sunbeam's next-door neighbor, Mr. Charlie. His yard was teeming with beautiful Jamaican fruits and vegetables of all sorts. He raised Scotch Bonnet peppers, bananas, coconut, akee, callaloo, grapefruit, Jamaican apples, oranges, and star fruit, just to name a few. He was always proud to show us the fruits and in true Jamaica style, use his large machete, to intricately cut up any produce large or small to give us a sample. It always took me aback when, accepting an offer of a small piece of fruit, Mr. Charlie would demonstrate his finely tuned cutting, chopping, and slicing skills with a large machete as if it were a small paring knife. But best of all, Mr. Charlie loved the Sunbeam boys. It is almost as if, in them, he saw his own children or perhaps he saw himself as a boy. He was gentle and respectful with the boys and gained our respect the first year we met him.

Both of my children, having seen how much I loved traveling to Sunbeam Children's Home, had expressed the desire to travel with me sometime to experience it firsthand. 1999 was the year for my son, Sam, as a junior in high school. Two of his friends also came with us that year. What a treasure it was to witness their relationship-building with the Sunbeam boys and their willingness to jump in and do whatever was necessary. Sam, Cole and Mike worked on a project involving digging up the present drainage pipe, unclogging it, repairing it, and digging a new trench. Much to the team's amusement, the boys described this difficult and smelly project as "really fun." Just guessing, but I am thinking none of them would have used these words to describe such a task if it were asked of them by Dad and Mom back at home in Minnesota.

It truly was a difficult task, working in the rocky clay soil with shovels all day long. They worked with the less-than-desirable tools. *"Yuh cyan tie up a dog wid sausage chain"* (You can't tie up a dog with a chain made of sausage) (McLean, 229). It's hard to do tasks with inappropriate tools. Sometimes using tools that are not optimum for the situation cause the job to be more complicated or take longer. But, despite that, and with the hot Jamaica sun beating down on them all day, the boys completed their job and they smelled like sewer rats, but they were smiling sewer rats, nonetheless. They chose joy.

The Sunbeam boys love it when we bring teenagers with us, as the boys relate to the visiting teens easily and are so eager to make those connections. The Sunbeam boys, knowing I was Sam's mom, continually asked, in their Jamaican accents, "Where's Som?" "Is Som sleeping? "When will Som be ready to come out?" "Can I help Som?" "Is Som finished eating?" "Can Som play outside with us?" It is difficult to tell who was experiencing more joy: me, as "Som's" mom, the boys, or Som himself.

An amazing thing happens when you bring along a bunch of awesome people, each with their own skills, talents, and life experiences, who all share the common goal of making the lives of our Jamaica boys better in some way. Over the years our teams have included people in many of the trades: electricians, carpenters, auto mechanics, machinists, and welders to name a few. And we have brought social workers, ministers, high school students, college students, chemical dependency counselors, and teachers of all types. Musicians, insurance people, bankers, truck drivers, business owners, homemakers, and retirees have joined us. We have brought medical doctors, nurses, veterinarians, veterinary assistants, and occupational therapists. The list seems never-ending. The most wonderful thing about this wide variety of people is that the team is well-prepared to tackle about any work project that we are asked to accomplish at Sunbeam. And these folks do it with a joyful heart. One does not sign up for this gig without a willingness to answer God's call and do whatever needs to be done. They embody the old Jamaican proverb, *"Walk better dan sidong"* (To walk is better than to sit down) (McLean, 7). Sitting and watching a situation doesn't get the work done. Diving in and doing the work gets things done.

One of the advantages of Sunbeam Children's Home being owned by a non-profit corporation is that larger, wider scale work projects can be shared, with multiple groups tag-teaming onto each other's work to get the greater goal accomplished. Charlie, a member of our church as well as a board member of Sunbeam's non-profit owner, coordinated much of the work projects for us, communicating with the board to coordinate with other groups regarding needed work projects. With large projects such as the new water collection and filtration system, one group would work on a certain aspect of the project and the next group would pick up where the first team left off. Charlie is a well-respected fix-it guy for almost any planned work project or request that came up while at Sunbeam.

The most striking thing about our team members who worked on all the projects, big or small, is that they did it with joy in their hearts. When it came time at the nightly team meetings to talk about work projects, I don't recall even one time in twenty-five years that when there was a job to be done the next day, more than one person didn't jump in and say they would do it. It was so heartwarming to watch them work, usually without the modern tools and methods they were accustomed to using, sometimes in scorching heat and humidity, and having things take twice or three times as long because of the "extra help" from little boys who so wanted to be a part of the action. Our men and women served as role models for these kids, and understood that, in the eyes of the boys, they were the father, mother, big brother or big sister role models that the boys so longed for but perhaps did not currently have in their lives.

Sometimes a tool was laid down and the next time it was needed, it was nowhere to be found. Sometimes it was discovered that a critical part of the job could not be done without a run to the hardware store, which could delay the project for an entire day. Sometimes things had to be jerry-rigged or short-cutted to make them work. Very often it was one step forward and three steps back. Punting was a way of life.

The very first year our church went to Sunbeam, I somehow managed to volunteer to reupholster a blue faux leather couch. The fabric had completely worn off the arms and seat cushions, and the back of the couch was threadbare, basically unusable. This occurred before the current benches were built, and other than a few random beat-up wooden chairs, there was no furniture in the big gathering area except when the dining room benches were carried out for use. My upholstery experience? Zero. Upholstery experience for my upholstering partner, Grandma Jean? Zero. But we decided to give it a whirl, only to hit a dead end when we discovered there were no tools to complete such a job. Had we known about this project, we could have brought the appropriate materials with us from Minnesota, but it was one of those requests that came once we arrived, a frequent occurrence. So, it became a matter of "fake it til you make it," similar to a Jamaican proverb that states *"Tek whey yuh get tell yuh get whey yuh want"* (Take what you get until you get where you want) (McLean, 274). There are going to be disappointments, setbacks, and downright failures, but just maybe you'll eventually get there.

We gave Pastor Lue some cash, with instructions to find upholstery fabric and a staple gun, two items essential for the upholstery job. I had found a measuring tape, a dull scissors, a large needle, thread, and a hammer in a locked cabinet in the dorm. What more could I possibly need for such a job? Pastor Lue found some fabric, a dark maroon crushed velvet—a bit over the top, but OK, it would work—and I did my measuring and cut the pieces that afternoon. Finally, a staple gun arrived late in the afternoon the next day, with only one more workday prior to our departure. I tested the staple gun and it worked about every third try. Good enough.

With the help of several of our boys, we pulled the couch out onto the front yard and worked where the sunlight provided us a better place to see what we were doing, but a bit uncomfortable in the hot Jamaica sun. Grandma Jean and I spent about six hours cutting, stretching, and stapling before we declared it complete. Eager little helpers made the job larger and frankly, more difficult, but that time with the boys was priceless. The little helpers felt proud, as though they had a part in providing a soft, comfortable place for them and their brothers to sit. We dragged the newly reupholstered couch back into the living room, and everyone wanted to sit on our masterpiece. It was a big job, but we sure had fun. I was not surprised to witness, that evening, eight skinny little Jamaican boys sitting on our beautiful new couch all at one time. In my mind, I gave that couch a life of about two weeks before it would be completely trashed, simply from overuse and lack of care. Much to my pleasant surprise, when I returned two years later, the upholstered couch was looking a bit tired, but it was intact and still in use. Score!

In 1997, we arrived on the scene to find a garden tiller that we were told had been sitting in the corner of the living room for two years because one of the tires was bad. Matt, one of our young team members, happened to work in a tire installation and repair shop and had the skills to repair the tire, so it was fixed, out of the living room, and making the job of the resident farmer easier out in the garden by the end of the day.

It is always dangerous making lists. But in reviewing my notes from twenty-five years of Sunbeam visits, it is interesting to read the lists of the team's accomplishments. Listed are just a few of the hundreds of projects, to give the reader an idea of just what we do! They are in no particular order.

- Built wooden storage cabinet for school room and filled it with supplies
- Installed clothesline poles
- Put a stucco finish on the dorm addition
- Made curtains for the women's dorms
- Built, painted, and installed screens in wooden screen frames throughout the entire building
- Built the foundation for the farm hand's house in Sunbeam's backyard
- Repaired pigpen gates
- Organized a numbered box system for the boys' clean clothes
- Repaired all the boys' school uniforms
- Purchased washing machine, had it delivered, and installed
- Repaired laundry room door
- Made welding repairs on the stainless steel sinks in kitchen
- Painted shutters
- Installed three large water collection barrels
- Tore out and built a new soffit on one corner of the roof
- Scrubbed kitchen cabinets and put contact paper on the shelves
- Put new chicken wire on the security doors
- Constructed a bathroom, from plumbing to framing to installing fixtures
- Installed new frames and doors for the men's and women's dorms
- Installed metal grate over one of the basement-level windows
- Repaired water leaks in the water fountain, sinks, and toilets to reduce the monthly water bill

- Installed new zinc on the lean-to laundry room
- Moved food storage to a different room by gutting, installing ceiling, painting walls, and installing a metal door and lock to the new area
- Extended the eaves on the fowl coop to increase the shade inside for the chickens
- Broke out the old and poured new concrete in the boys inside shower room, re-tiled
- Did some post-hurricane roof repair on Miss Ivarene's home
- Secured the roof tin on the main building roof with screws; patched holes in dorm roof
- Installed shelving in the ironing room
- Brought and distributed 110 flannel blankets to the younger boys and to surrounding communities
- Built large benches for the gathering space. Repaired and painted benches in subsequent years
- Taught animal husbandry skills to the animal caretakers, and conducted necropsies on chickens who had died
- Maintenance and repairs on the water collection and purification system
- Painted the boys' dorms and every single nook and cranny of the building—multiple times

"Wha' noh pisen, fatten" (What does not poison you fattens you) (McLean, 16). Every experience, including digging sewer trenches, performing autopsies on chickens, and repairing pigpen gates, has some good in it. An important lesson: find the joy. Embrace it. Positivity brings energy, a sense of hopefulness, and a brighter outlook.

Chapter 8

Lesson: Take Care of Yourself

No one ever claimed this missionary stuff was going to be easy. There is so much that goes into the preparation, fundraising, and organizing, not to mention the matter of organizing one's home and work life to prepare for being away on mission, a matter easier for some than others. Add to that the hard work comes in the middle, while in Jamaica. Yes, there is hard, physical work for a lot of us while there, but so much other behind-the-scenes work that goes on which challenges us in so many ways. And then there is the time when we return home to decompress and process, while catching up with our home lives and families and return to our paying jobs. No matter how hard it is in that middle time, it is always worth it, whether it is in the short run or in the long run. But it is all work, and one must put in the work to reap the benefits. *"Victarey nuh cum fram lie dung eena bed"* (Victory doesn't come from lying in the bed) (McLean, 309).

Sometimes it has been frustrating to me, over the years, when I get the inevitable, "Must be rough—Jamaica in January!" or "How was your vacation?" Most people do not understand mission work, really. I did not, either, until I did it. It is not a vacation. It is not lying on the beach. It is not staying in a resort hotel in the tropics with hot showers and fresh towels every day. It is not standing on the corner preaching. It is not a rescue mission. In our case, it is building relationships, and doing physical labor projects that make the daily lives of our Sunbeam boys a little better than they may have been before.

We live in a busy world. We have all reached the point where a few minutes of quiet time in the morning or evening does not quite give us the rest and relaxation we need. There are times when we are exhausted physically, emotionally, and spiritually. These same things happen to us in Jamaica, too, and they often feel like they are magnified in great proportions. The team meetings and a night in the bunk provide a sense of renewal that help us deal with that.

But we still run out of gas at times. I am retired now, but during my working years, running out of gas was a daily thing during the peak of my career in higher education. I remember reading a timely devotional one evening during my years serving as the Vice President of Academic and Student Affairs at a two-year college in Minnesota. It was the end of a long and stressful workday of problem-solving and multiple people issues, and I was completely exhausted, in every way a person could be exhausted. Fittingly, my devotional for that day stated that maybe God wants us to run out of gas occasionally so that we will crawl up into his lap. He longs to love and comfort us and too often we ignore how much we need that. If there is one verse in scripture that I have focused on many times in my life is Matthew 11:28: *"Come to me all who are weary and burdened, and I will give you rest."* I am woefully inadequate when it comes to Biblical scholarship, but this one verse I know and have practiced during the challenging times in my life. Once we slow down and take time to comprehend that, we can relax and allow the words to re-energize us. At Sunbeam, our days are filled with joy and laughter and satisfaction. But at the same time, those days are usually challenging and complex, with perhaps a few added layers of heightened emotions and often, dehydration and sheer physical exhaustion.

More than once, I and others have crawled up into God's lap to feel his presence and comfort. There, we rest, regroup, and help each other find the exhilaration and energy to move ahead. We always find it.

Slowing down and consciously taking care of ourselves is the only way we can be of any value to anyone else. *"Empty bag cyan stan' up"* (An empty bag cannot stand up) (McLean, 126). The first year I went to Jamaica, Patsy and I and a few of the other team members spent a day at Strathmore Children's Home, as documented in Chapter Two. I had come to Strathmore that day because I had felt compelled, a few days prior, to give these kids some human interaction and human touch. I could sense such a terrific need for holding and hugging and smiling. So, Patsy and I did that all morning. I scooped up kids by the armload and we brought them out to the climbing structure which was built by another visiting Minnesota team in the recent past. I had brought some bubbles with me; the kids loved them. We read them stories and sang songs. The names I remember are Peter and Paul (brothers), Big Jason, Little Jason, Duane, Jonah, Ainsley, Trisha, LaToya, Wayney, Scotteesha, Gaffey and Little Georgie. I wrote about Jonah in Chapter Two. There were many more. Frankly, we needed bigger laps. The kids listened quietly and respectfully to the stories. They crowded in to see the pictures in the book, and their curiosity made them repeatedly but gently touch our skin and hair, enthralled with its color and texture, much different than their own.

Patsy and I had a memorable experience at lunch that day which was one of the more difficult things I have done, ever. We had locked our thermal water container, lunch, and other supplies in Sister Williams' office earlier in the day so that they were secure. All the windows in the facility were the wooden louvered-type windows that were always cranked to the open position to allow as much air flow as possible in the warm and humid Jamaica climate.

When we had a moment to eat, around one o'clock, Patsy and I went into this office and closed the door to sit down and get a drink and eat, since we were getting very hungry, as well as dehydrated from the heat. We had prepared peanut butter sandwiches at Sunbeam that morning before leaving for Strathmore. We sat down in that office, and within moments became aware of a gathering of children outside the window, as they had followed the sound of our quiet conversation. Soon little outstretched arms and hands, with palms up, were poking through those louvered windows amid the sounds of "Please, mam." "Please, mam." The kids were hungry, and they were begging for food.

In an awkward moment, we put the food away, looking at each other, thinking "How can we possibly eat?" We sat for a while, wondering what to do, discussing the situation. Finally, Patsy said something akin to, "We know we have to eat. We are not accustomed to this schedule, this heat. We have to take care of ourselves and stay hydrated." So, we did eventually get out our water and peanut butter sandwiches and ate. My sandwich was stuck in my throat. I have never enjoyed a meal less.

Only later in the day did we learn, through observation, that the kids at Strathmore ate only once per day, around three o'clock in the afternoon. They have tea in the morning, then no other food until their three o'clock meal. So, about the time we were eating our peanut butter sandwiches, the kids must have been at one of their hungriest moments of the day, and there we were, eating within an arm's length of their outstretched hands. I know that we had to eat and drink, as our bodies were accustomed to doing. I know that logically. But that moment haunts me to this day.

Taking care of ourselves took on many forms. From the very beginning, we built a "pilgrimage day" into our schedule as part of our mission experience. It provided a respite from the physical work we were doing, while at the same time giving us a broader Jamaican experience as we saw, experienced, and learned more about Jamaican culture, health care, leisure, education, social welfare, and even food. It gave us many experiences to reflect on and grow in our faith journeys. In the twenty-five years of mission trips, we visited nurseries such as Glenhope and Marigold in Kingston; Strathmore Children's Home; a senior care facility; a Food for the Poor warehouse and distribution center; a women's clinic in a neighboring town; the Promise Learning Centre for children with autism; Spring Village Community Center; Spring Village Primary School; and Heroes Park in Kingston. There are so many more. And we hit some splendid beaches like Hellshire Beach in Kingston, Doctor's Cave Beach in Montego Bay, Seven Mile Beach in Negril, and Lime Cay off the coast of Port Royal. We tasted Jamaican patties, oxtail, jerk chicken and pork, curried goat and other Jamaican goodies in restaurants and food stands throughout the countryside. And we bonded as a team as we climbed Dunns River Falls, traveled through the Jamaican countryside in our minibus, sat in Jamaican classrooms, and laughed at the signs in public parking lots reading "Please do not urinate here!" We even bartered for Bob Marley beach towels, Blue Mountain Coffee, and bamboo banks at the Kingston Craft Market.

We often began our pilgrimage day with tours of various facilities such as the ones mentioned above, sometimes bringing gifts and supplies such as diapers and blankets, school supplies, or medical supplies. It provided us the opportunity to learn more about Jamaica, but also to share ourselves and bring a little joy with us. We were always met with open arms and big Jamaican hearts, and we came to understand the kindness, loyalty, and easy-going nature of the Jamaican people.

The Golden Age Home became one of the highlights of our annual pilgrimage for many of us. Golden Age was established to provide care for any adult in the Kingston and St. Andrew parishes who was destitute due to age, illness, cognitive or physical ability and was unable to work to earn a living to support themselves. It was built on a four-acre plot in 1982 after a catastrophic 1980 fire at its original location in which 150 elderly women tragically perished. There are groups, or "clusters" in which six resident buildings are built around a quadrangular courtyard. There are eight such clusters.

Cluster G, where we spent most of our time, housed many adults with physical and cognitive disabilities of all sorts. The setting was beautiful, with a giant magnolia tree in the center of the courtyard. We made our way around to each room, greeting each resident, sometimes singing with them, and happened upon a retired opera singer, who especially enjoyed singing along with us and even performed for us. She was nearly blind, and age had taken its toll on her voice, but the pure joy of singing and performing briefly took hold of her and it was a beautiful thing to see. The residents so yearned for and appreciated the touch of another person, and when we did so, smiles lit up their otherwise emotionless faces. I distinctly recall a woman sitting on a bench outside her room, with a blank look on her face. I sat down beside her, slowly moved in for a big ol' hug, and got the biggest toothless smile you can imagine. Despite her frail appearance, she had a hug that could "squeeze your guts out", as my young son used to say, and she had no interest in letting go for quite some time. So, I went with it. We then sat together for quite some time, and I had a one-sided conversation with her. She never said a word—I think perhaps she was not capable—but she never quit smiling the entire time. I could feel her firm grasp on my hand linger as I stood up and told her I needed to move along and catch up with the rest of the group. The firmness of that grip made me sad.

One of my favorite photos taken during that trip shows Pastor Keith bending down close to an elderly woman, their hands clasped with each other's, Keith's eyes locked with hers. Another one shows Jennifer leaning closely over a woman lying in a bed, their hands in a four-hand embrace and eyes locked together, wide smiles on each face. In another, Claudia and a little sprite of a woman sit close, all hands entwined, with both of their heads thrown back in laughter. There were a thousand moments like this through the years at Golden Age Home. At every turn, the storyteller in me wishes I could know each person's story and give it the life and spirit it deserves.

One year we visited the Promise Learning Centre, a school for children with autism aged five to eighteen. The sign on the outside of the school states "Every child has the God Given Ability to Achieve." In pairs, we chose one classroom and sat for about an hour observing and assisting when needed. Maureen and I were in the toddler room. It was an emotionally exhausting visit, but so interesting and so satisfying. Stories about some of our nursery and children's home visits, where I had so many awesome experiences, appear elsewhere in this book.

Our visit to National Heroes Park was unique and touching in a different way. The Park is located in Kingston on the land formerly known as the Kingston Racecourse, the largest open space in the city. The City of Kingston bought the land in 1808 for the racetrack, and it was the center of horse racing in Jamaica until 1953, when horse racing was transferred to a different location. Cycling and football (what we North Americans know as soccer) were also held there at various points in its history. After Jamaica's independence in 1962, the Jamaican government decided to create a permanent place to honor the country's national heroes. The Park was then renamed National Heroes Park, and monuments were erected in honor of Jamaica's seven national heroes in an area known as The Shrine. Adjacent to The Shrine is a section reserved for the interment of former Prime Ministers and others who have contributed to the political, educational, and social development of the country. We witnessed the formal changing of the guard. What I found most meaningful at this stop was to watch the extreme pride and reverence that Pooh and Marla exhibited as they spoke about this place and explained the significance of these seven heroes to their little island's story:

> *Sir Alexander Bustamante* – Activist against colonial rule and former Jamaican Prime Minister
> *Marcus Garvey* – Political activist; founder and first president of Universal Negro Improvement Association (UNIA). Believed that black people must work toward becoming financially independent in a country run by white people
> *George William Gordon* – Businessman and politician critical of colonial government
> *Norman Manley* – Statesman; first Premier of Jamaica

> *Nanny of the Maroons* – Eighteenth Century leader of a mountain community of formerly enslaved Africans. Led several battles against the British
> *Samuel Sharpe* – Slave; leader of the Baptist War slave rebellion in Jamaica
> *Paul Bogle* – Jamaican Baptist deacon and activist. Leader of the 1865 Morant Bay Protestors, who marched for justice and fair treatment for all people of Jamaica, but especially the poor.

It is admirable and inspiring to me that the people who were chosen as Jamaica's heroes were those who actively fought, even back as far as the eighteenth century, against colonial rule and the treatment of black Jamaicans as less than those of the white ruling class. It reminds me of the similar struggles we experience in the United States even today.

Pilgrimage Days could be physically and emotionally draining at times, but they also provided a wonderful opportunity, in the early days, for rejuvenation in the middle of the week before heading back to Sunbeam to finish up our work projects. In more recent years, we scheduled this pilgrimage day at the end of our mission experience to serve as a means of relaxing, debriefing, and learning more about Jamaica while beginning the transition back to our lives at home in Minnesota.

One day in 1997 our Jamaican friend Michael, who accompanied us on our bus adventures on the island in those days, told us of a "mineral spa" which would cure all that ailed us. Michael told us he would drive anyone who wished to go visit, and that it would only take about a half hour to get there. I announced this opportunity to the group and opened it up to anyone who wished to go, feeling that a short afternoon break from our work projects would be good for us and would provide an opportunity to see more of the island. After all we could, according to Michael, be there and back in about an hour and a half. Ron, Patsy, and I decided to go, interested in this [tongue in cheek] marvelous cure. We decided to bring a suitcase full of small toys and treats and stop in one of the villages and distribute them to any curious children who gathered.

Though only forty-five minutes late, on time by Jamaica standards, Michael came to pick us up around one o'clock in the afternoon and off we went. In those days, I was the cook for evening meals, so I left recipes and instructions for meal preparation, *just in case*. What we did not realize ahead of time was that Michael had a few errands to run along the way including, as I recall, picking up some hair extensions for his sister or girlfriend, I don't remember which. Additionally, he did not know or remember exactly where the agreed-upon location was to pick up the said hair extensions. We stopped in a small settlement and enjoyed distributing small pocket toys to local children; think Matchbox cars, McDonald's Happy Meal giveaways, and small plastic animals. A few wrong turns, miscellaneous other errands of Michael's, and a grossly miscalculated total mileage meant a two-hour trek to the "mineral spa," but we finally did arrive.

Patsy and I had been expecting a lush, tropical spring bubbling out of the earth, with outdoor pools teeming with bubbling hot water, like what one might see at the Blue Lagoon in Iceland. Suffice it to say that our expectation did not match with reality. The rundown indoor baths reminded me of solitary confinement prison cells, not that I have first-hand knowledge. Each bath consisted of a cubical, tiled room of about ten feet by ten feet, in which one enters by walking through a lockable door. Within that small room, one walks down concrete steps into the water and sits on a built-in, tiled, concrete bench in the warmish water, about chest deep. Ron, Patsy, and I had put on our bathing suits under our clothing prior to our departure, so we just took off our outer clothes and walked down the steps and submerged ourselves, awaiting our miracle cure. It was a bit comical given our initial expectations, but the fellowship was great, our conversations echoing off the walls of this confined space for about a half hour. An hour-and-a-half trip home meant we ran in as supper was being served back at Sunbeam, five hours after we left. When it was all said and done, we felt terrible about abandoning our team for that amount of time, but in terms of self-care, even though any claim of cures for arthritis or any other malady notwithstanding, it was a wonderful little get-away that provided good camaraderie, stress relief, and a lot of laughter.

I did some informal research among my Jamaican friends after the fact about the Milk River Baths, to find out more about this interesting place. What I did not know at the time was that the Milk River is the main source of water for the Clarendon Plains area in which the baths are located. The mineral waters flow out of the earth and claim to help those suffering from things like arthritis, rheumatism, and various other medical conditions and honestly, whatever one thinks might ail them at the time. The temperature of the water is about ninety to ninety-five degrees. The secret, evidently, is that the water contains high levels of chloride, magnesium, calcium, and sulphate. The waters are apparently somewhat radioactive. Now, as in much of Jamaican history, these "facts" were passed down from generation to generation and eventually to me, so may or may not be embellished or true or partially true, but I have chosen to take them as mostly factual. My recent online research bears this out.

And true to Jamaica's preference of oral as opposed to written history for recording its past, there is a legend associated with the mineral bath that dates to slavery in Jamaica. A slave who worked for a plantation owner in the area committed some sort of offense that resulted in a brutal beating with severe injury, and the slave was locked up in a dungeon. He was somehow able to escape the dungeon and run away and was then miraculously healed of his wounds by bathing in a warm spring. Several days later, he returned to the plantation to convince his friends and loved ones to run away with him.

Word about this miracle cure got to the slave owner, who promised to free the slave if he told the owner the location of the spring. The slave brought the owner to the healing spring, and the owner subsequently purchased the land around it and established the Milk River

Baths in the late eighteenth century. The owner eventually turned over the property to the Jamaican government so that the Jamaican people could enjoy it and benefit from its healing powers. A century or two later, Ron, Patsy, and I were three "Jamaicans" who were able to enjoy this place thanks to this runaway slave.

Lesson: take care of yourself. There may be roadblocks and detours along the way, but always remember that you're worth taking care of.

Chapter 9

Lesson: Be Patient

"*Patient man ride dankey*" (A patient man rides a donkey). This Jamaican proverb (McLean, 72) reminds us that sometimes the steps we take are small ones, but they are indeed steps. Donkeys are slow and can be a bit ornery but will get us there most of the time if we persevere. Sometimes we must get off the donkey and yank the stubborn beast forward. Sometimes the donkey may make a complete stop regardless of our efforts, and perhaps even buck us off the saddle, if we even have a saddle to cling to. But we get back on and persevere.

While it seems that so many of the life situations I encountered among the children of Jamaica seemed hopeless, patience seems to be innate in nearly every Jamaican's temperament. There is a reason *"No Problem, Mon"* is a widely heard sentiment in Jamaica. This lesson learned in Jamaica is one that I particularly needed and found most important. There were examples every single day showing me Jamaicans, young and old, modeling patience in situations that would probably crumble me to bits in a half a minute if I were to endure them myself.

Siblings Shanika and Fabian, ages five and seven at the time and residents of Strathmore Children's Home, were scheduled for a court hearing to determine if they would become wards of the government or if they would be sent back to their family. They had been bathed and dressed that morning in the finest clothes the staff could find in the pile of communal laundry so that they would look as presentable as possible for their court appearance in Kingston. They were beautiful kids, giddy with excitement about the possibility of going back home, despite the crowded, squalid living conditions to which they would likely return. These children wanted to go home. It was all they knew, and that is where they would find the only mother they had known.

After being occupied with other children most of that day, I noticed by mid-afternoon that Shanika and Fabian were in their play clothes. I asked Miss Williams if it was possible the children had already gone to Kingston, appeared in court, and returned. As it turned out, their ride never came to pick them up. That one act of forgetfulness, car trouble, miscommunication, or lack of attention to detail changed the course of those two little children's lives. So that was that. Life in Jamaica. Shanika and Fabian did not make their court date. They could conceivably wait an entire year, maybe more, maybe never, to get another court date. Until then, they would be at Strathmore or another children's home, awaiting whatever direction their lives would take them.

The dashing of hopes after a long wait seems to be accepted as a fact of life for the children in Jamaican children's homes. I will never forget driving away that first year I visited Sunbeam in 1995. My little friend Omar was so afraid he would miss saying good-bye to us before we got on our bus at six o'clock the next morning that he stayed up all night. For a time, I wondered if it was worth it to put these boys through the emotional roller coaster of having such a great week, only for them to have to say good-bye a relatively short time later. The little ones would cling to us the last few days, knowing our departure day was approaching. The older ones would become more reserved and retreat into their thoughts when the time came closer. I would think of the routine to which they would return, and the hopelessness that some of them would again feel.

But over many years of missions, I have concluded that letting these boys know that someone in the world cares about them is worth it. It was worth putting them through the parting process. There were few dry eyes in the crowd as we drove away that first year in our bus to the sound of their appreciative clapping, and shouts of "good-bye, friends, we love you." So many of these boys had said good-bye so many times, had waited for people to come back so many times, had waited for the pieces of their lives to make sense and to fit together, and were disappointed again and again. It was not surprising that, even though we said we would be back, they did not believe us. Another person, and yet another and another, was leaving them behind.

In later years, these boys learned that these whiteys from Minnesota and other places did indeed come back again and again, and over time, the older boys would let the younger ones know that we would return. I realize now that our repeated returns have given something quite valuable to these boys, and that is *hope*. We would be perhaps the first people in their lives that would come back. Their wait—even for an entire year between our visits—would not be in vain.

Another area in which we learned to practice patience was in the farming operation at Sunbeam. When Pastor Lue, Sunbeam's founder, purchased the five-acre plot of land many years ago for the boys' home, his dream was to grow crops on the tillable part of the property so that the boys could learn how to farm and, in the process, supply the home with nutritional meals for the boys.

Through the years, Sunbeam hired farm workers and managers to work the farm toward that end. And visiting mission teams built hog, goat, and chicken facilities to add to the working farm. One year a few of us planted tomatoes all week. There were so many tomatoes later that year that Sunbeam was able to use what they wanted and sell the extra ones to others. Lettuce, callaloo, and cucumbers were planted at different times through the years and used in the Sunbeam kitchen, and bananas were harvested from the trees on the property. Grants were received for various agricultural projects. But the operation was never as successful as Dr. Lue had envisioned. Sometimes it was weather issues and hurricanes; sometimes it was personnel-related; it just never seemed to go gangbusters. What is interesting is that the general lack of agricultural success at Sunbeam mimics the country's agricultural conundrum.

Agriculture is one of the major bases of the Jamaican economy, accounting for about one-twentieth of the GDP (*Gross Domestic Product*, the total value of goods and services produced within a country in a specific time period) and about one-sixth of the workforce (5/6/20 Britannica.com/place/Jamaica/economy). The major crop is sugar cane [and its byproducts, such as molasses and rum], and fruits such as oranges, coconuts, and bananas. Minor products include squash, coffee, allspice (pimento), cacao, fish, tobacco, and ginger. A frustrating irony for Jamaica is that it is a fertile land with the ability to produce an abundance of fruits and vegetables but is increasingly reliant on cheaper agricultural imports, driving the country's farmers out of business. With Jamaica importing foods easily grown on the island, its government has been trying to invest in a more self-reliant agricultural economy in recent years, with programs that promote urban gardening, school-run garden projects, and increased banana production for export to the European Union. This has only been marginally successful, as Jamaica continues to import most of the food it consumes, thus keeping rural farmers poor. With foreign products flooding the market, Jamaica increases its exposure to the whims of international markets and jeopardizes its own food security. So, defying logic and opportunity, agriculture has been a struggle in modern Jamaica, just as it has been at Sunbeam.

A grant was received in the early 2000s to build a hog facility at Sunbeam that would generate enough manure to convert to methane gas, which would then be used to power Sunbeam's kitchen. One hundred and fifty pigs would be needed for the system to be sustainable.

When our team arrived at Sunbeam in 2014, there were two groups of new piglets and several pregnant sows. Animal husbandry skills would be needed to keep these pigs thriving and ultimately build the numbers. Unfortunately, it just did not happen.

One of the first nights we were at Sunbeam in 2014, a pack of dogs got into the fowl coop and killed most of the chickens. So, we got busy the next morning and secured the fowl coop against predators. It takes two hands to count the number of times we rebuilt or upgraded or fixed the fowl coop and bought new baby chicks to kickstart the operation again. One year we tried again, ordering chickens in advance and our faithful driver, Patterson, drove up one day with a trunk full of 300 chicks and several bags of feed to get them started. Another year, we constructed different rooms within the fowl coop: one for new chicks, one for fryers, and one for layers. For periods of time, the chickens were well taken care of, and Sunbeam was supplied with eggs and even sold the extra eggs to outside customers. Emilio, a quiet and responsible older boy at Sunbeam, was charged with taking care of the chickens and picking eggs for a period of time, and things went relatively smoothly. Then, there were other times when the chickens were not well taken care of, or the door would be left open, or it was too hot or too cold, or predators got in. These and any number of other issues resulted chicken operation stops and starts again and again.

We were fortunate to have a veterinarian on our mission team on two different occasions, and during one of those visits, Dr. Al was called in to action to respond to some mortality issues with Sunbeam's chicken population prior to our visit, and egg production was way down. Much to the attentive interest of many of the boys, Dr. Al pulled up a barrel as a tabletop, got out his instruments, and conducted necropsies on a few of the chickens to see if he could determine the cause of death.

There were "walls" on the fowl coop that could be placed over the screen material to protect the chickens from rain or other weather conditions. As it turned out, the weather had been cooler and the boys had been cold, so they decided the chickens must be cold, too. The boys had rolled down the side walls of the fowl coop, essentially creating a heated oven inside the coop. The chickens became stressed from the heat, and many died as a result. Once Dr. Al was able to convince the boys that the chickens were too warm, the health of the flock improved greatly, and egg production rose to previous levels.

In 2014, a twenty-year-old college sophomore from a college in Vermont was doing an internship at Sunbeam for his major in Land Management and Sustainability. He stayed in one of the apartments in the twin home on the property, and stayed for several months, including the time during which our team was at Sunbeam for our annual visit. Klaus was a good-natured, easy-going guy who appreciated having us around as much as we enjoyed and appreciated having him around. His primary task was to get Sunbeam's land ready for planting in the upcoming season.

At the time, we had great hopes that Sunbeam, with its chickens, pigs, crops, and new water retention and filtration system, would become increasingly self-sustainable. Things went smoothly for a while when Klaus was present, as he stayed on top of the hard work that farm management requires. But history repeated itself once again when Klaus left, and without the constant attention, strong work ethic, and farm oversight every single day, it once again fell into a less than effective operation.

Patience isn't for wimps. It often grows with age, maturity, and insight. As Americans, we have often had to leave our Type A, intense, time-oriented productivity-based inclination behind when we travel to Jamaica, and instead put on our patient pants. Patient pants have certainly been needed when it comes to the farming operation. However, past frustrations have led to a new greenhouse on the property financed through a grant, producing cucumbers, peppers, pumpkins, and okra. The produce helped reduce food costs and added healthy foods to the boys' menu. Like so many other things, however, the grant monies expired and there is no one to manage the greenhouse operation. As a result, its use is minimal, and its future is unknown. Further complicating things was a major flood of the area in the summer of 2021. One step forward, five steps back.

Another area which necessitated our patience was the kitchen. Every year in memory, as mentioned previously, our team brought kitchen supplies of various sorts to supplement Sunbeam's disappearing-or-breaking supply. Silverware, plates, small appliances, pots, pans, utensils. One year, we were fortunate to score several sectioned lunch trays from the local elementary school that had closed in our small Minnesota town. These things were heavy duty, childproof trays that were designed to withstand the toughest child and the constant commercial dishwashing. And in the following years when we returned, we found that most of them were gone. It takes a patient heart to come back every year and understand these situations.

Patience. A characteristic inherent in the Jamaican culture, but not so with us. The constant challenges we encountered gave us countless opportunities to practice patience at Sunbeam Children's Home.

Chapter 10

LESSON: TAKE CARE OF EACH OTHER AND ALLOW OTHERS TO TAKE CARE OF YOU

THERE WAS A time when, looking back, we really created quite a disruption for the boys in the evenings at Sunbeam Children's Home. We always had an evening program with lots of singing and laughing and roof-raising. No problem there, other than riling up the boys to the point that it would have been difficult for them to get to sleep immediately. But then, we would do some sort of project with the guys, such as making a friendship bracelet or decorating t-shirts, or something similar. The boys were so wound up by the time we were done that they didn't get to bed at a reasonable time, even on school nights. All in all, it really wasn't very smart of us. The boys loved it, of course, but we completely threw off their bedtime routines. Royally. It was unfortunately fitting, as there was little leadership, discipline, or consequences for bad behavior in those days. Boys were allowed to stay at Sunbeam until well after they were 18, so often were out and about in the neighborhood, coming back late at night and causing trouble. Sometimes under the influence of alcohol or gangi, they would act belligerently or even beat up the little guys. The younger boys would tear around and refuse to settle down. It must have been a nightmare for the overworked and underpaid house parents.

In recent years, under more structure and discipline, the visiting teams are asked to be out of the gathering area by eight o'clock in the evening, when the house parents then engage the boys in their bedtime routine without the distraction of guests. At that time, the team retreats to the basement school room for a team meeting.

In the team meeting, we talk about our day, decompress, and debrief, have a short devotional of some sort, and plan for the next day. How did you spend your time today? How did it go? Got any suggestions for dealing with Jermaine? Everybody feeling OK? Anything you want to share tonight? What supplies do we need? Does anybody need help with Project A tomorrow? Who wants to walk to the corner for eggs and blue paint? Who's on five o'clock a.m. kitchen duty? What's our schedule tomorrow? Do we need extra kitchen help for dinner tomorrow?

Nightly team meetings are very practical things to do, but their greater value probably lies in the opportunity to release some of the emotions of the day, tell one's stories of the day, and rely on each other's common experience and support to process it all and be better prepared for tomorrow. This is especially important for those team members who are experiencing Sunbeam for the first time. It's overwhelming. I saw it repeatedly: first timers spent the first few days in a suspended state somewhere between shock and disgust and sadness and excitement and joy. The culture shock is very real for those who have not visited third world conditions. It's like emotions on steroids.

One year we brought along a grandma whom I will call Ruth. So many of the Sunbeam boys were raised by their grandmothers before they came to Sunbeam, or at least lived in multi-generational homes in which their grandmothers were present and influential. So, grandmothers often elicit feelings of *home* and *warmth* and *comfort* for the boys in perhaps an otherwise complicated life, and they gravitated toward our team members who were of that age group. Ruth was a rock star. In between kitchen duty and other projects, she would sit out in the living room and chat with the kids. There was always a lively conversation going on, perhaps a smaller boy on her lap, perhaps a teenager sitting by her side, leaning in. She was a daycare provider back home, so was well-versed in the kid skills department. Ruth smiled a lot, had a hearty laugh, and talked about whatever the boys wanted to talk about. She could have a verbal contribution on most any topic. She listened to what the boys had to say and allowed them to lead the conversation.

Once, near the end of the workday as we were cleaning up before dinner, I happened to come upon her leaving the women's dorm. As she turned around, I could see that her eyes were filled with tears. I gave her a hug and asked her what was wrong. All she said was, "I miss Paul." Paul was her husband, whom she had lost in the prior few years.

Ruth was a first timer at Sunbeam. All of us who have been to Sunbeam have been first timers at Sunbeam. It can be overwhelming. The extreme range of emotions in the first few days had just caught up with Ruth: the living conditions; the bug bites; the heat; the physical exhaustion; and all of this layered on top of the heartache and sadness of the boys' life stories and realizing the hardships some of them face every single day. All these things create a smorgasbord of emotional highs and lows that can sometimes, out of nowhere, take us to unexpected places. The emotions of the day had given Ruth the realization at that moment that she would be unable to share these intense and beautiful experiences at Sunbeam with her lifelong soulmate whom she had just lost.

We talked it out for a while, and she was back to herself before too long. As the leader of the team and a veteran of the emotional experiences that come with short-term missions to places like Sunbeam, I felt the responsibility to give team members the opportunity to share and to receive support from the others, so I encouraged this at our nightly team meetings, and Ruth did so that evening. It allowed us to give her our support, as well as perhaps validate the same emotions that others had been feeling. The lesson it taught me was that it is healthy to share our struggles and allow others to help us through the challenging times. This is something that I had not been particularly good at through my own life, and a lesson I needed to reinforce.

Team meetings always ended with a prayer, led by whomever felt the urge. And to close, it was always an a cappella version of "Lord, Prepare Me to be a Sanctuary." It was important for us to "be a sanctuary" for each other, providing a place of retreat, protection, restoration, strength, and healing. The team meeting was a time where we took the necessary time to be that for each other. This is something that, unless you have been involved in the mission experience at a children's home in a third world country, may be difficult to understand.

Each time we travel to Jamaica, we are equipped with a theme for the week, which had been decided quite early in the preparation cycle and was then reflected in our team t-shirts and our programming plans. One night in the early 2000s, we were focusing on how Jesus had taken care of our salvation and how he continues to take care of us. A team member whose name I won't share, but will instead call David, shared the story of his involvement in the Viet Nam war and how he came back and became addicted to street drugs and alcohol to cope with the emotional after-effects of the war. He shared that he had been sober for twenty years and how it was his faith that pulled him through that time in his life. The boys were captivated by David's story. I was so proud of him for this forthright and heartfelt presentation, and for the effect it had on the kids. It was striking to me how the comfort and familiarity and safety of David's fellow teammates and their support of him allowed him to share such an intimate detail about his life.

When it nears the end of the week and we must think about leaving Sunbeam, many of us reflect not only on the boys, but on our teammates. When a group spends six months or more planning and preparing, then lives together in those conditions for even this short while, they grow very close. They have experienced emotions together and shared things with each other that wouldn't necessarily be shared in other circumstances. I think also of another team member's revelation of alcoholism earlier in his life, and the comfort he had talking about it with us. Emotions are sometimes raw, as our comfort with each other allows the outer layers to be peeled away as we experience and speak of things that we've never experienced or spoken of before. It truly is an amazing, supportive environment.

There has not been one year when I have not been truly proud of the people who chose to embark on this adventure, just for the people they are. Each night, we go to bed not really knowing what the next day will bring. We get up and we deal with whatever happens, and we deal with it with adventurous, cheerful hearts. Damien ruffles Steve's hair, sticks his finger in Steve's ear, and Steve just laughs. Kids pile around Cindy as she sits at her sewing machine, begging to use it themselves so they do, and break a sewing machine needle. Cindy just smiles and puts in another. Kemanie grabs Brooke's camera and tries to snap a picture. She smiles for the picture and gently takes the camera back. One of the boys picks up a power tool laying in the basement work area. John calmly tells the boy to put it down and pats him on the shoulder as he tells the boy of the danger. Fran dishes up lunch onto the boys' plates as several are crowding around her and grabbing for food. She smiles and calmly tells them there is enough for everyone. Even as a veteran team member, I am constantly overwhelmed with the richness of this experience year after year. These are all moments that helped teach me the lesson that we need to, and do indeed, take care of each other.

Kirk loved to take care of us. He had been a Sunbeam boy in the past. It was the only home he really had as a child. He was born with some physical limitations, but made up for it with a joyful, willing, generous heart, relishing most the role of helping others. He grew up and aged out of Sunbeam but continued his connection by working odd jobs there for several years, ultimately being tasked with helping Sunbeam prepare for visiting mission teams. He made the dorm beds prior to the teams' arrival, made sure there were towels for everyone, swabbed the dorm floors, and coordinated some of the teams' needs while at Sunbeam. He was happiest when knowing he was helping others; and beamed with pride when his hard work was acknowledged. Kirk embodied the old Jamaican proverb, *"Visitors come a wi fireside, wi mek wi pot smell nice"* (When visitors come to our home, we make our pot smell nice) (McLean, 28). He made our dorms and bathrooms sparkle prior to our arrival, giving the best of himself to welcome us to the place that was his home for many years. We grew to love Kirk's deep-voiced, "Yeah, Mon" and charming smile. He was proud to share with us that he was so trusted at Sunbeam that he had a set of keys for the facility, a responsibility given to very few.

Kirk lived at Island Farm, a local settlement, in a house provided by Food for the Poor. His home had been damaged by a recent hurricane and had only been partially restored when we visited it in 2009. The little home was modest—one room with a bed, chair, small electric refrigerator, and some storage containers—but it was Kirk's home, and he was proud to live in it, an opportunity not available to all young Jamaicans.

Tragically, this faithful servant died of cancer in October 2019, while only in his forties. When I think back on my many years at Sunbeam, Kirk's face shines bright in those memories. He was instrumental in teaching me that it is important that we take care of others and that we do so joyfully.

Damien, O'Shane and Germaine found themselves at Sunbeam Children's Home in the late 1990s, when a staff member found them huddled together, sleeping, near the riverbed in the far back boundary of the Sunbeam property. It took some research on the part of Children's Services to determine that these boys were just three of their mother's eleven children. They were pushed out onto the streets because there was no more room in their house and no resources available to feed them. When the three boys arrived at Sunbeam, they were initially more comfortable sleeping together in one single bed with their backs touching each other, most likely the way they had protected themselves and kept themselves warm while living on the streets of Jamaica. Eventually they all moved into more age-appropriate dorm rooms at Sunbeam and over the years, adjusted relatively well.

Damien, the oldest of the Miller boys and about six feet tall, had some cognitive and learning disabilities and probably a variety of other developmental issues that Children's Services felt may have been caused by head trauma, most likely abuse or assault, as there were several visible scars and indentations in his skull. He was able to count and say his ABCs, but unable to put letters together to form words. He was emotionally and intellectually immature for his age. The staff believed that, while at Sunbeam, he spent much time in the neighbors' yards smoking gangi, one of the only ways that Damien could perhaps feel a sense of relaxation and well-being. Damien was a busy guy, a bit hyperactive, loved to tease, and was extremely good-natured. With the physical presence of the older boys and the intellectual and emotional maturity of the younger boys, he mostly kept to himself in the beginning, not fitting in either with the bigs or the littles.

Middle sibling O'Shane was a pleasant, caring person who especially enjoyed helping Mrs. Bryan in the kitchen or helping farmhand Lucky with the farm work. His softhearted nature manifested itself in his love for taking care of the dogs and cats. It was thought that, because of his slightly nasal voice, he may have had a slight hearing loss, again because of possible head trauma of some sort.

Little brother Germaine seemed least affected by his former life on the streets. He had an engaging smile and loved gymnastics and karate and kick boxing, anything in which he could display his athletic talent. His insatiable appetite and previous life circumstances caused food insecurity problems which manifested themselves in intense greed and food hoarding. It improved over the years as he gradually learned that there would always be another meal at Sunbeam.

The amazing thing about oldest brother Damien was his interaction with his brothers. One day during our 2003 visit, Pastor Corey observed Damien interacting with his two brothers and mentioned how heartwarming it was to see Damien turn from the goofball that we all knew, into a nurturer. Damien had assumed the role that he played for many years prior to their arrival at Sunbeam: that of protector and mentor to his younger brothers. In this case, he was speaking to O'Shane and Germaine about something, and he spoke in a fatherly, responsible, tender way that just didn't seem to be the Damien that we knew. No young boy of Damien's age should have the responsibility that he had for such a long time. It is awesome to think of God giving Damien whatever tools he needed, even with Damien's limited capabilities, to take care of his brothers for however long he had to until their lives got better. Another lesson learned: God provides us what we need when we need it.

"Wan han wash de oda" (One hand washes the other) (McLean, 263). The spirit of cooperation is innate in most of us, and is applicable to our work lives, our family lives, and in our actions with others in all other aspects of our lives. This spirit of cooperation among mission teams becomes essential in the short-term mission experience. It's difficult to get through life without helping each other out: a lesson that seems so simple, but that has a profound effect on the quality of the experience as well as the end game.

Chapter 11

Lesson: People Suffer in God's World

"Di daakes' part a di night, a when diay soon light" (The darkest part of the night is just before daybreak) (McLean, 11). Life for many children in Jamaica requires resilience. It requires faith, toughness, and sometimes, courage. This is no different than is the case in many third world countries. However, for many of us on short term missions to Jamaica, it is the first time we witnessed firsthand these types of life hardships among its most vulnerable. It is difficult to see, but also necessary to see, because it puts names and faces on poverty, hunger, and hopelessness. One does not leave Sunbeam Children's Home without some serious reflection and adjusting of one's perspective. When times are the toughest for the children, it is sometimes being placed in a children's home like Sunbeam that begins to instill a small ray of hope. They may go from being homeless or being in an abusive home to a place in which they are fed three meals a day, have a ready-made clan of brothers, and in an environment where hope prevails. As McLean states, "When times are hardest, bright times are sometimes near."

The first year in Jamaica, team member Matt was paired up with Sunbeam boy Michael, age nineteen. When Michael was four years old, his mother took him with her to the market, went home, and purposely left the market without him. Michael never saw his mother again. Four years old. Think of a four-year-old that you know, maybe your own child as at age four. Michael survived on the streets, as many other children do. He stole food and got by as best as he could. Once he was caught stealing, and the punishment deemed appropriate for him was to get his thumb cut off. He lived on his own for his entire childhood, eventually finding an old abandoned, gutted bus, which he called home.

That bus happened to stand in the backyard of what would become the current Sunbeam Children's Home property. When Sunbeam Children's Home was built, they took Michael in. He was about fourteen at the time, so had been living on his own for ten years. He lived at Sunbeam until not too long before we arrived in 1995, when Michael found his own home.

Michael was excited to show his new friend [team member] Matt his new home. Having one's own home is something that is not common for young Jamaican men. Matt reported that Michael's home was a small one-room shack with a metal cot. Matt could stand in the middle of the home, hold his arms out straight and touch the walls on either side. A board would be propped up in front of the doorway to "close the door."

Michael had not been at his new home for very long, and still hung out at Sunbeam a lot, so he was included in our activities and was treated as one of the boys. He relished the camaraderie and friendship of Matt. Michael had suffered much in his short life, and experienced things most of us cannot even imagine.

In one of our trips to Sunbeam, Little Kemanie had arrived on the scene immediately prior to our team's arrival. He was nine years old and had come from a horrific ghetto area in Kingston. He was noticed by two office workers whose hearts went out to this skinny little boy as they saw him begging on the street. It was not known at the time how long Kemanie had been in the streets, but it was later determined that he had been badly beaten and sexually abused when he lived at his home.

When he first came to Sunbeam, Kemanie wet his bed every night. How I agonized over watching that sweet little boy drag his mattress outside to dry in the sun in the morning, then drag it in at night. He got mercilessly teased by the older boys, and I recall several times when his bedwetting resulted in severe reprimands from the Superintendent of Sunbeam, a military man who did not last long in that position.

A year after Kemanie arrived, I saw no indication of a bedwetting problem, and I always hoped that was the case. I would like to think that, even though it will always be a part of his life, the trauma he endured in his early life was fading from his memory and that he was becoming more comfortable and accepted at Sunbeam. After three years at Sunbeam, I found Kemanie to be a polite and shy little boy who loved to play cards as well as help with the chores. He clearly had a road still to travel in dealing with his past and with his progress in school after a slow start in life, but he was making progress. Sometimes that's all we can hope for. He seemed to be a natural leader and had so much potential. What a joy to provide this sweet and loving boy to a special day at the beach with our group, as well as many special treats tucked into his outstretched hand during the week.

Where is Kemanie today? I have often wondered if he truly was able to overcome the incredible challenges of his earlier life and make a new life. Children should not have to endure the things this little boy had experienced.

An encounter with another little boy, George, put a face and a name on the human suffering that so often accompanies children who live in poverty. My first experience with George was my first year in Jamaica, 1995, as the entire group toured Strathmore Children's Home for the first time. In those years, the home was in desperate condition, as were the children who lived there, and as I mentioned previously, has made significant improvements since that time. We initially visited this home to check up on a piece of playground equipment that had been constructed in the front yard by a previous mission group, and to look for potential future projects. I did not know what to expect and was not prepared for what I would soon see as we walked through the facility. We slowly walked through the converted residential home as Sister Williams, an elderly Jamaican woman, showed us the place.

I passed a crib in one of the bedrooms which was metal, with paint chips peeling off. I envisioned small children peeling away each chip and placing the paint chip in their mouths or worse, chewing on the sides of the crib and ingesting the paint chips. On the bottom of the crib was a piece of plywood with rough, uneven edges. The plywood was blackened in places, stained and dirty. No mattress, no foam, no blanket. This was where a child slept, his or her soft skin against the jagged, splintering plywood. It was hot there, very hot. And humid. There was no water that day in January. The electricity wasn't working. The two toilets in the building had overflowed at some point earlier, and water from them ran throughout the building. Children sat on the concrete floor in the back of the building, many of them sitting on round plastic bowls—the kind you or I might use for cereal—as their toilets. Other children sat in the eating area on a long wooden bench, some with little to do nor the strength or motivation to even eat. There were no toys. They sat and stared at us or some other unidentifiable point. There was a stench of urine. And it was dark, everywhere. Empty light bulb sockets within the reach of children in the top bunks were devoid of light bulbs. The bunk beds were packed into the bedrooms so that ten to twelve children slept in each room. Some of the beds had mattresses and sheets, but both were dirty and stained and smelled of urine. Beds were, in some cases, just mattresses covered with plastic and no sheet. The windows, wooden louvered slats which opened and closed, were mostly broken, permanently affixed in either an open or closed position.

Some children sat in the "backyard," a four-foot-wide strip of concrete bordered by a concrete brick wall, over which was strung a few lines of barbed wire, serving as a place to hang wet laundry. Garbage was thrown over this concrete wall into a swampy area. Kids sat out here on the concrete area in the hot sun, for hours, until someone came by and picked them up. They did not cry; they just sat.

Overwhelmed, silence overtook our group from Minnesota as we walked through Strathmore. Over the years, it has brought more than one to their knees in tears or a delayed reaction with no sleep the following night. My initial reaction was to avoid touching these kids with mucous-encrusted faces, skin conditions, and urine-soaked clothes, always with no underwear, and often no pants at all. It is everyone's first reaction. But I felt overwhelmingly compelled to do so, because it was obvious that this is what the children needed most. As I picked up a few, I could feel them nestle and mold themselves to me: head on my shoulder, hand on my back, face in my chest, bodies curled into a fetal position. The few staff members at the facility barely got them fed and the laundry done. It wasn't their fault. There was little time for hugging. Children ran their hands through our smooth, Caucasian hair in amazement and comfort. A fear of strangers, especially white strangers in those days before it was commonplace, was eclipsed by the children's need for human touch.

It was this environment that a little boy named George called home. We walked through this home and, as I passed through the eating area where the kids sat and ate from a plastic bowl full something I could not identify, one little boy stood out. This little boy, whose name I learned was George, sat at the table, staring at each one of us as we walked by, as if to beg, "Please help me." He had the saddest eyes I had ever seen, with dried on mucous covering his face. He had on a tattered t-shirt and nothing on the bottom half of his body. It was heartbreaking. He sat by himself, as if shunned by the others, though I do not know if that was actually the case. After asking Miss Williams his name, I went up to George, addressed him by his name, and though I did not get a smile in return, I did receive an acknowledged look that I preferred to think meant, "thank you for speaking to me." Sister Williams informed me that George could neither speak nor walk. That was our introduction.

Two years later in 1997 when I returned to Strathmore, the change in George, whom I hadn't dared think could get any worse, was stunning. He was sitting alone out next to one of the small outside buildings, again only partially clothed. At first, I wasn't sure it was him, but that haunting little face, crusty scalp, and aimless stare gave him away. I didn't think he could get any skinnier or unhealthy looking, but that was surely the case. I remember wondering at the time how he could have survived the two years since we had last met. I have a photo of George taken that January in 1997, curled up awkwardly on a homemade bed consisting of a wood frame with wooden slats. No mattress, no blanket.

I knelt beside him, told him I was "Miss Heidi," the accepted way to address a woman. And even though there was no verbal response, he seemed to soften somewhat and did not cower when I sat down on the concrete right next to him. So, there I was, sitting next to George. I read him books, I blew some bubbles, and carried on a one-sided conversation. I talked about my kids. I talked about flowers and trees and sunshine and clouds and things that I thought he might know about. I want to believe that, even with his limited cognitive capacity, he somehow knew that the voice he was hearing, even if the words may not have represented anything sensical to him, was a friendly one.

In 1999, I returned to find George in a similar but weakened condition. He had spent most of his time lying on the floor inside, or on the gravel outside, quietly moaning or crying. He was a small package of skin and bones, so fragile. I again parked myself next to George on the floor, hoping the sound of a soft, reassuring voice would at least soothe him, if nothing else. I stroked his cheek and again spoke to him about anything I could think of. He quit moaning during that time. I said a prayer out loud, hoping God could somehow find a way to spare this sweet young boy his pain and suffering.

When I returned to Strathmore in 2000, I immediately checked with house mother Isabel about how George was doing, now five years after I met him. She knew from my repeated visits that I had grown attached to George, and she seemed somewhat befuddled by my interest and the attention I paid him. When she told me that George had died during the past year, my heart sank and rejoiced at the same time. It saddened me profoundly and made me reflect on what God had had in mind for this short life, perhaps eight or ten years long. I hope that I had made some minute difference in George's life. I hope that, like Jonah, somehow George could draw strength from the few moments each year that I spent at his side, talking softly and stroking his cheek. I have wondered many times if anyone was with George when he died. Or did he have to do that alone, too?

What drew me to George? The same thing that draws me to every little child in Jamaica, regardless of circumstance. We are all equal in God's eyes. My childhood Sunday School song sticks in my heart, "Red and yellow, black and white, they are precious in his sight. Jesus loves the little children of the world." Strathmore's children are just children born to different circumstances than most of our own children. George was a child of God, equal in God's eyes to my own kids. George's life was of no less value. I wanted someone to care about these kids as much as I cared about my own.

George's legacy? I am not sure, other than the profound effect he had on me. He is the one child in Jamaica that flies through my consciousness more often than any other. But I envision a healthy little boy, dancing his way through heaven right now with fully functioning arms and legs, an extended family full of people that love him, friends to play with, a full stomach, and a soft bed.

One day while visiting Strathmore Children's Home in 1998, I met three sisters, Tanya (age four), Tomika (age three) and Trisha (age eighteen months). They had come to live at Strathmore sometime during the preceding year. Like many families in Jamaica at that time, their mother did not live with their father. The little girls had been staying with their father in a very small, crowded shack, because their mother was pregnant and hospitalized with complications related to her pregnancy. While the girls were living with their father, his house burned to the ground. The kids escaped unharmed, as did their father. But the father, with no other family to lean on, had no place for the children. So, he delivered them to the doorstep of Strathmore Children's Home saying he would be back to get them when he could. He never came back.

One of the older girls at the home, Shanika, age twelve, had gotten quite close to the three little girls and I noticed immediately that she was the person who comforted the three little girls when they needed it. If one of the other children picked on Tanya, Tomika or Trisha, Shanika was right there defending them and consoling them as she wiped away their tears. I am sure that this gave Shanika a purpose in her life, and it may have been lifesaving for the young girls.

On this visit I brought fifteen bedsheets which we had carried to Jamaica in our suitcases from Minnesota. In addition, we had a large bag of Children's Tylenol, cough medicine, and diarrhea medicine. Miss Williams was overwhelmed with this gift, and in fact began to softly cry when she received these gifts, stating that this was an answer to prayer. I watched as she took each box or bottle of medication and placed it in a locked medicine cabinet in her office, which previously contained only one lone bottle which appeared to be a prescription medication for one of the children. The Strathmore medicine cabinet was now full to the brim. She stated, also, that for a long time, there had not been enough sheets for all the children. As a result, some slept on a bare mattress or a plastic sheet like a shower curtain draped over the metal bed frame, wooden slats, or springs, as we had witnessed.

There were only two workers in the home the day we were there, and apparently, they were the only two employees there, other than Miss Williams, the director. Cynthia, a middle-aged woman stated that she had worked at Strathmore for 16 years, and that she stayed there all day and most nights. She cooked for the twenty-five to thirty children and did her best to tend to their needs. The other worker was a slight woman named Cherise. She appeared to also do some direct care of the kids. But there simply were not enough arms to go around. Sister Williams, the director, spent some time in the office when she was there, but was perhaps in her late seventies and seemed quite frail at this point, not able to physically assist with the children.

Cynthia and Cherise did their best to meet the children's basic needs with the few resources they had, but the need for nurturing and physical touch was not met to any appreciable degree. It is no wonder the kids clung to Shirley and me as we held them and hugged them, read them stories, colored with them, and sat on the ground and played. When we held them, they nestled right into our necks and pressed their bodies against ours, as if to touch as much of the surface space of their bodies against us at one time as was physically possible. I remember hoping at the time that somehow these kids could memorize the feel of those hugs and the security of our arms around them and draw on that memory as the year passed by before we would see them again.

I am amazed by these children's stories. Every child seemed to have a story of overwhelming loss or abandonment or sadness. What took some adjustment on my part was to first notice, then understand, why these kids did not cry much at Strathmore. I have noticed this in other children's homes, also. They have learned it does no good. They cry, but nobody comes. It is important to note that this does not necessarily indicate a lack of caring and compassion on the part of the staff members; those staff members are simply overwhelmed. It is an impossible situation.

I developed an intense interest in this children's home from the very start, as mentioned previously. As I later served as a leader on these mission trips, I always made sure that our Sunday afternoon drive included a stop at Strathmore. Some of our team members had to stay in the bus, as it was just too difficult to witness the conditions in which these little children were living. I understood this and did not force anyone to go anywhere in which they were not comfortable.

Another little girl at Strathmore captured my heart and broke it at the same time. As the team stopped by Strathmore in 2000 after our Sunday morning church service, I came upon a small child as I was making my way through the dark and dank hallways of the home. The child, a girl, was lying awkwardly in a small, yellow, plastic oval-shaped wash tub, lined with what appeared to be a plastic cloth like a shower curtain. I was horrified not only at the sight of this little girl, but also at the thought of the physical discomfort that she must have felt, in a stuffy building in ninety-plus-degree heat, lying directly on plastic in her own urine. I compared the size of the tub with the size of the blue metal tub that my mother used for kneading bread in when I was a child, perhaps twenty-four to thirty inches long and twenty inches wide. The child fit into the container with her skinny, misshapen legs and arms bent up in unnatural ways to conform to the confines of the plastic tub. Her muscles were flaccid.

I thought that this child, whose name I learned was Melinda, was perhaps a very handicapped two- or three-year-old. I was shocked to learn that she was eight years old. I sat in that room most of the time the group was touring Strathmore, gently rubbing Melinda's cheek with the back of my hand, trying to elicit a response from her. I gently lifted the bottom of her loose, tattered shirt and saw her protruding ribs, each one easily visible, and a rapidly rising chest with each labored breath. She had no diaper on and no clothing from the waist down, the reason for her bed of plastic, I presume. Her cheeks were sunken, and her teeth protruded awkwardly from her mouth, seemingly too large for her emaciated little face. This was truly one of the saddest situations I had come upon in Jamaica up until that point. I could elicit no response in Melinda. Her eyes were closed and remained closed. I could only hope that she had no sense of her surroundings.

I will never believe that suffering is a punishment for sin or that the amount of suffering is somehow proportional to the amount or magnitude of our sin. My simple mind cannot explain why God allows suffering. God certainly didn't keep a scorecard on Michael, Kemanie, George, Tanya, Tomika, Trisha, and Melinda on which the sins outweighed the good deeds. All I can understand is that God stands by our side when we do suffer, and always hears our prayers when we cry out to him. So, I continue to pray for these and all the other children of Jamaica who are suffering.

Chapter 12

Lesson: We Share the World with God's Creatures

A COMPILATION OF stories about my travels in Jamaica cannot go forth without giving attention to the critters that we encountered. In all cases, they were not the kind of critters that one needs to spend a great amount of time worrying about; however, when a Minnesotan travels to a rural location in a tropical third-world country, there are bound to be some chance meetings that produce some momentary discomfort.

On our very first visit, in 1995, we received a great introduction to the creatures with which we would be sharing Sunbeam Children's Home. On Sunday morning, we had to brush away the roaches and other crawling bugs as some of us stood making toast. The home did have working electricity most of the time. But if toast was to be made, which was not frequently, it was made in quantities that were not practical by using a typical toaster. Instead, bread was buttered and then fried on a griddle. The toaster was mostly reserved for visiting mission teams. Hence, the toaster had become the comfortable home of several species from the insect world between those visits. As soon as the toaster heated up to a temperature not habitable for such critters, they scurried out across the kitchen, seeking alternative digs. That year, we also continually brushed away cockroaches—yes, some the size of mice—that came up through the cracks in the tables to investigate the food we were eating.

One of our missionaries had a close and personal critter incident that has given us much laughter through the years. She was a senior citizen that we will call Bess (name changed to protect the innocent). Bess and a few other of our team members, along with a few of the older boys, were playing cards late one evening in the large common area of Sunbeam. This was back in the days where we visitors only wore skirts when on the property, appropriate for Christian women at the time, out of respect for the Jamaican culture. In the middle of a card game, Bess felt something moving on her upper leg, dangerously approaching the underwear zone. With lightning speed, she grabbed her skirt at the precise location and trapped the moving critter in the cloth of her skirt with her hand. But then what?

Bess had no choice but to pull up her skirt and reach under with her other hand to grab the critter and shake it out onto the floor. It turned out to be a large cockroach. Excitement, screaming, embarrassment, and raucous laughter ensued, but the highlight was perhaps one of the boys' unabashedly loud comments, "I saw Granny's bloomers!"

One evening not long after we found cockroaches in the toaster, some of us noticed a rat in our suitcase storage area. It was also not uncommon to spy a rat running along the upper edge of the concrete blocks of our dorm or dining room, up near the ceiling. It is hard to imagine this becoming routine, but it truly was in those early years, until we made improvements in the structure that kept most of the rodents out, or at least invisible to us. As recently as 2018, however, we ran into rat issues again, as one or more had managed to chew through the ceiling and come down into the pantry. The rats ate all of the bread, as well as anything not secured in a tin or plastic bin. We went to work repairing the ceiling and securing all food items by putting them in rat-proof containers. Charlie did not make the situation any better for us Minnesota missionaries by repeatedly planting a large plastic rat on the top of the concrete block of the shower stall in the women's dorm. The rat has made so many appearances over the years that we should know better, but it always gave us a jolt.

In 1997, I was exposed to a little more wildlife than I would have desired. I woke up one morning at four o'clock to a bat which had dropped down onto my pillow. I brushed it off, not knowing what it was at the time due to the darkness, and not really wanting to know. I figured it was probably one of the many small lizards that resided in the home, a large cockroach, or a bat, and neither of the three was a particularly palatable thought, especially when realizing we were sharing a pillow for a moment. At any rate, with a vigorous stroke of my hand, I brushed it off, flinging it to who-knows-where, and fell back asleep.

Within a few moments, I heard a blood-curdling scream come from Mary's bunk next to mine. She jumped up from her bed, no words, just screams and gulps of air. She clearly had been awakened from a deep sleep. Flashlights came on within seconds, creating a laser-like light show, with beams seeking the source of whatever Mary was screaming about. The entire women's dorm was awake, not knowing if we were dealing with a medical emergency, a critter, or a Jamaican ax murderer. Honestly, all I really wanted to do was go back to sleep, after only having finally gotten to sleep around one o'clock a.m., only three hours prior but clearly, as the team leader, I felt I should probably do something about whatever was going on.

The ceiling light was turned on and, apparently temporarily stunned, a bat was perched on Mary's bed, right next to her pillow. After much deliberation by many, a suggestion from someone to "whomp" it, an objection from one of our teenage team members to "let it live," as well as some miscellaneous screaming, laughing, and carrying on, Mary said, "Heidi, I need you to take over here." So, I promptly shined my flashlight on that rascal and whomped him with the bottom of my sandal one-two-three times. At that point, Mary said, "Hit him again; he may be playing possum." So, after three or four more shots, I was satisfied he was dead, scooped him into a plastic bag which I then deposited outside our door, and went back to bed, thinking I would deal with it the next day, but wanting to just get it out of the sight of the women at least for the night. I must admit that I am now feeling a bit guilty about choosing that cruel method of ending that bat's life. I mean, what a terrible way to go. But at the time, I felt the need to take control of the situation and get everyone calmed down. Mary and Patsy spent the remainder of the night with their sheets over their heads, their flashlights in hand, and their eyes wide open. I laid there, awake, until light, around 5:30 a.m. Another short night, and another adventure to talk and laugh about the next day and long into the future.

That same year, I found myself with the task of cleaning the area around the garbage dump in the backyard, pitching garbage into a large hole dug by a backhoe which we had hired to prepare the foundation trenches for another building. We had the backhoe remove the current garbage pile and dig a large hole for a new one. While cleaning up garbage, I encountered quite a bit of Jamaican wildlife including large cockroaches (two to three inches long), a few small lizards, and many scorpions. The type of scorpion that lives in Jamaica can be up to six inches and have large litters of babies that ride on the mama's back for eight days before they hop off and terrorize the world all on their own. Apparently, they often live in the walls of houses or under rubbish piles. I have seen them in both places at Sunbeam. Jamaica's Professional Cricket League team is "The Scorpions," so I guess these ugly creatures are not viewed with the same fear and repulsion as I seem to think is warranted. And they do scarf down all the cockroaches in sight, so I'll give them a few points for that. I escaped any scorpion stings that day in the garbage pile and every year since but seeing this number of scorpions in one place motivated me to move from bare feet or flip flops to tennis shoes, no matter where on the property, from that point forward.

One night in 1998, we had a lively night, seemingly common in those days, and it resulted in everyone having critter phobia. Becky and I took Kathy's backpack out into the hallway after narrowing a "mouse noise" to that area, and a little mouse jumped out and ran across my foot! After that, everyone seemed a bit rodent-shy. Once that happened, every small noise during the night was met with a flood of flashlight beams. I admit that listening to the little nibbling and scurrying sounds of mice was a bit disconcerting at times, but I think I could have slept just fine if not for the middle-of-the-night flurry of screams and flashlights and miscellaneous humans jumping out of beds at astounding speeds. Cindy seemed particularly overwhelmed by the prospect of seeing a mouse, and Patsy had the remarkable ability to fall asleep with her finger on the ON button of her flashlight.

That night, as I woke up around four o'clock a.m. for a bathroom break. I didn't want to turn the light on in the bathroom, since the bathroom walls did not reach all the way up to the ceiling, thus showering the sleeping area with light. Everyone needed their sleep, and I didn't want to be the person that took it away from them. Upon entering the stall, I saw a critter of some sort dart out. I am not a screamer, but my heartbeat was screaming. I do not know what that critter was, but perhaps it was better not knowing. My guess was a mouse.

Goats are everywhere in Jamaica. As we arrive on the island and exit on the airport road, goats casually graze alongside the road. As we travel through the countryside, over mountains, through forests and gullies, and alongside the ocean, goats walk alongside the road or can be seen perched atop piles of rubbish on the street corner. Goats pass by Sunbeam on the side of the road on their way to or from somewhere, or during the nighttime, make their way to gardens containing good munchables not always accessible during the daytime hours. Individual goats, goats in herds. Random roads and busy highways. I am constantly amazed that there aren't dead goats strewn everywhere along the roadways, kind of like the dead deer that frequent the roadsides in our area of western Minnesota. There always seems to be a frayed rope tied around these goats' necks, hanging freely or dragging on the ground, as if they just made an escape from wherever they were once contained within a yard or fence.

When we see goats in our neighborhood at Sunbeam Children's Home, the locals can tell us where each goat belongs, and not to worry—those goats will make their way back home tonight or tomorrow. Goats are raised in Jamaica primarily for their meat (goat sausage, goat burgers, goat ham), and to a lesser extent, for their milk, cheese, yogurt, and skin care items such as soap. Curry goat is a fixture on the Jamaican menu, often served with rice and peas, roasted breadfruit, or plantain. Goats even make their way into the wonderful Jamaican proverbs such as *"If you wan' milk, feed de goat."* (If you want milk, feed the goat). Translated: One must give in order to receive.

In 2016, I had a wonderful sleeping spot in the dorm, or so I thought, located in a corner where there was a window on each wall, allowing a wonderful Caribbean breeze to blow through, right across my face. What I didn't factor into the equation was the fact that the screens were full of holes and as a result, it was a prime spot for mosquitoes to fly in from all angles to seek warmth and escape the cool night air. Imagine their pleasure when they found me there, an evening snack. I received multiple mosquito bites throughout that night and many others. I came home that year covered in bug bites, only to learn that the Zika virus, spread by mosquitoes, had recently been found in this as well as other parts of Jamaica.

As it turns out, according to Jamaica's public health agency, the first case of Zika virus in Jamaica was confirmed on January 29, 2016, with date of onset on January 17, the very week we were at Sunbeam. Between January and July, there were over four thousand cases of Zika recorded. (https://www.ncbi.nlm.nih.gov/pubmed/28375542). I am happy to report that I did not contract the Zika virus, and instead just did a lot of scratching.

Friday, January 17, 2003, was fire ant day for the team. Al discovered that the ants had come marching in two by two right into his bedsheets. They were everywhere. His bed in the men's dorm was in the same position as mine was in the women's dorm: right along the wall in the corner. I thus expected that this was a sign of things to come for the women's dorm, also. I can deal with fire ants. I had already been bitten numerous times on my feet and legs due to wearing sandals instead of tennis shoes. But I preferred not to sleep with them.

The bedsheets got thrown out into the outdoor laundry room, a trip down to Gutter's Corner in search of powdered insecticide for the ants became my mission for the day. I was successful, with Al sprinkling the contents in both rooms, which solved the problem for the week. "The Fire Ant Blues," a song improvised by Corey and Dwight, was a hit at the evening program.

Critters! They all have a purpose, and we must share our world with them. There are many opportunities in a third world country to do so.

Chapter 13

LESSON: LET GO

IMMERSION INTO THE boys' living environment as we do when in Jamaica, our team has a unique opportunity to develop very close relationships with the boys. We are with them when they get up in the morning and we are there when they go to bed at night. We see the ebb and flow of their daily lives, the good, the bad and the ugly. We see them interact with the Sunbeam staff and their Sunbeam brothers. Some of it is pretty; some is not. We hug them, play with them, eat our meals with them, sing with them, dance with them, and worship with them. We come to trust them as our protectors as we travel out in the community. By the end of our time in Jamaica, we have become so attached that we feel as if we are family—with the boys, with the staff, and with each other. How can that happen in a week, you say? Trust me, it happens.

In the early years, it was a tradition on the last night of our visit to gather as a team under the stars in Sunbeam's backyard after the boys had all gone to bed. We gathered in a circle and joined hands, reflected on our time in Jamaica, and served each other communion. It always ended, appropriately, with lots of hugs, which I always felt served as our affirmation of our teammates and our commitment to each other and to the work we were doing, as well as a good-bye. I think about the closeness that develops among a group of people in this situation, and all the wonderful people with whom I have shared this experience. There is always a deep sense of accomplishment, given the trying circumstances, the lack of tools and equipment, the hot weather, and with everything that is comfortable and convenient stripped away. Defying logic, it turns out that to be forced to rely on faith and each other is truly a wonderful thing.

I learned early on in this missionary thing the lesson of *letting go*. The words of a friend and fellow short-term missionary, Pastor Duane, got me through more mission trips than he ever knew. That first year, we had all gathered out under the stars in Sunbeam's backyard on our last night at Sunbeam. After sharing communion, Duane spoke to us all, saying, "We have done what we can do here this week. We have done an awful lot. We leave tomorrow, and the boys are in God's hands now. He will take care of them." If I did not have these words to hang my hat on every time I return to Jamaica, I am not sure how I would get through the experience time after time. My faith tells me that it is not up to me to save these children, but my passion for these boys makes it difficult to let go. I consider these boys my Jamaican sons, as do many of the others with whom I have traveled to Jamaica time and time again.

In 1999, I met a little girl named Shanique at Strathmore Children's Home. At the time of my visit, Shanique had only been there two days. She was nine years old and was very willing to tell me the circumstances of her arrival there. I asked her how she got there, and she said the police brought her there and dropped her off.

When she was living at her own home, apparently Shanique's mother beat her regularly, and at one time beat her so badly that she fractured Shanique's leg. Another time, her mother fractured Shanique's foot in a beating of some sort. After the second bone-breaking incident,

Shanique was sent to live with her father where, unfortunately, the physical abuse continued for this sweet little girl. Finally, someone intervened and notified the police, and Shanique was processed through the court system, removed from her father's home, and placed at Strathmore until she could be placed more permanently at another children's home for her own safety.

Shanique, a remarkably articulate nine-year-old, indicated she had never been able to go to school because "my mother wouldn't let me." I remember hoping against hope that Shanique would be provided, now in the children's home system, with the opportunity to go to school, all she ever wanted. The environment seems so bleak at Strathmore, but I suppose in the greater scheme of things, Shanique was better off than she was before. She would be given a meal each day, she would have a roof over her head, and I was confident that the children didn't get beaten there.

This was a situation, like a hundred others, in which there is simply nothing for us to do except provide some love and lots of hugs, and hope that we leave her with a memory that will allow her to understand that there are truly nice people in the world and that life isn't hopeless. Then, we hand her over to God. This is one of the hardest lessons to accept.

Given that we generally travelled to Jamaica during the month of January, I have had the wonderful experience of being in Jamaica many times on the day of my birthday, the 27th. My Jamaica birthday celebrations have included flaming cakes, a creatively decorated bunk, the creation of a well-endowed balloon woman under my covers as I returned from shopping, joyful "Happy Birthday" songs, gifts, and the Jamaican tradition of getting "floured" on my birthday. Yes, children and adults come running towards you and dump flour all over your head on your birthday and then laugh and point. One must just laugh along with them.

Another experience I distinctly remember on my birthday helped teach me the lesson to let go. Lori and I had the privilege of traveling with visiting Pastor Carol to Island Farm, a small, poverty-stricken village not far from Sunbeam. One must be prepared to witness extreme poverty when visiting this place. Our mission that day was to bring families clothing, diapers, food, and for the children, small toys, and a treat. Pastor Carol visited the village regularly, and the people there knew her and looked forward to her visits.

Another reason for our visit was to gather up the sickest of the children, load them in the van, and bring them back to Sunbeam, where team member Dr. Tim, a pediatrician, would examine the children and treat those that he could. What struck me the deepest was the willingness of the mothers to give up their children to us and watch us drive them away. They so desperately wanted their children to be well, but were powerless to do anything about it. The mothers handed their young children over to us, and we brought a van full of them back to Sunbeam. I remember thinking at the time that this meant we could easily have been exposed to any number of interesting diseases and conditions, but the overwhelming urge to help these mothers and babies took precedence. In a few cases, the mothers came with us; the others willingly handed over their babies, feeling a sense of relief, if only for a short while, from the burden of being unable to help their children feel better.

The central gathering area of Sunbeam became our clinic waiting room, and one of the boys' dorms was set up as an examining room. Lori and I bounced babies and toddlers as they waited to be seen by our doctor. One by one, the children were examined by the doc, often for the first time in their lives, and at the end of the afternoon, we loaded up the kids and brought them back to Island Farm, and once again, had to let them go.

This was the year we met little Aaron, whose story would intertwine with ours for years to come. While visiting Island Farm, we came upon a home where Aaron lived with his extended family. We told his mother that we had brought a doctor with our team, and that we would like to take Aaron back to Sunbeam, where this doctor would examine him. She joined us in the van with Aaron and, with the other children, we drove back to Sunbeam for the medical evaluations. Sometime in this process, I don't remember when, Aaron's mother handed him over to teammate Sara and asked her to keep him. His mother stated, "If you do not take him, he is going in the garbage."

We initially thought that Aaron appeared to be perhaps in the range of nine months to one year in age, as he laid limp in his mother's arms. He was very small and frail looking. His eyes did not track well. We were shocked to learn that Aaron was nearly two years old, specifically twenty-two months. We were initially told he possibly had a heart condition and seemingly had little chance of survival with the family's resources. And perhaps, even if the family did have the resources, the island did not have the medical expertise, equipment, and facilities that could save his life. Prior to our arrival, Pastor Carol had been bringing Aaron's mother baby formula, but his mother continued to feed him sugar water and bushy tea. "Bush tea" or "bushy tea" is made from the young leaves of Jamaican bitter melon. In Jamaican lore, the bitter herb is thought to be a blood cleanser and used to treat diabetes, hypertension, urinary tract infections, constipation, stomach pain, cold, and influenza. But clearly, Aaron was not thriving.

It was on this day that Sara, who was one of our mission group, formed a bond with Aaron that would not be broken. Clearly, Sara could not meet Aaron's mother's request to just keep him. We were flying back to the United States within days, and certainly nothing could be done in that short time to facilitate the removal of Aaron from his mother, nor any type of major medical intervention. Sara had no choice but to leave the country with our group and return home, leaving Aaron behind. She left with an extremely heavy heart. Would his mother literally put him in the garbage? Would he die from his illness? Sara felt she had imposed a death sentence on this little boy, and she couldn't stop thinking about him, even as she tried to transition back to life back at home. Her guilt prevented her from developing any of the photos from her mission experience or talking to anybody about her Jamaican mission trip for a period of time. She was deeply troubled, consumed by the need to help Aaron. As a person who was not comfortable flying and who generally became ill on most flights, Sara really had not known what brought her to the place in life where she was traveling to Jamaica on a mission trip. It's not something she would have naturally chosen to do. But this experience had helped her come to the realization that it was Aaron. Aaron was her reason.

Once back home again in Minnesota, Sara began researching the processes associated with bringing a Jamaican child to the United States for medical attention. It was long and complicated. It seemed there were roadblocks at every turn. She completed the required paperwork with what was then known as the Child Development Agency (CDA) in Jamaica and the U.S. Citizenship and Immigration Service in the United States only to find, when she turned it in, that other paperwork would be needed. Whenever something could go wrong, it *did* go wrong. Sara traveled back to Jamaica in 2001, to appear before a judge, personally turn in paperwork to the CDA, and do some other official business related to the process of bringing Aaron to the United States for medical help. Jamaica did not give up her children easily, even when it was in the best interest of the child. Visas were given primarily to those who were visiting family in the United States, or to children who would be educated or trained in a trade there with the intention of returning to Jamaica to benefit their home country. Aaron fit into neither of those categories. Sara was challenged at one point by having to answer the question, "Why do you want him?" She had a simple answer. She believed that every child had a right to live a healthy life. Aaron needed heart surgery and he could not get it in Jamaica.

Meanwhile, many events were happening in Aaron's young life. His young mother had died. He was subsequently placed at a children's home in Montego Bay. They did their best to nurture him, initially with the primary function being to figure out how to feed him. Because he had never learned to suck from a bottle, formula-type nutrition was initially given in quantities as small as a teaspoon, every hour around the clock. It literally took a matter of years to increase the amount to the point that he was getting the nutrition he needed to grow, and he eventually learned to drink from a sippy cup which, today at the age of 23, is still his preferred method of drinking. The children's home did the best job they could to help him survive, knowing that it might be in vain.

It took Sara four trips to Jamaica, thousands of dollars, and seven years to finally step on a plane in Montego Bay with Aaron in her arms, bound for Minnesota along with trusted friend Becky, also a short-term missionary from our church who had accompanied Sara on all her journeys to Jamaica. Along the way, bringing Aaron to Minnesota for heart surgery had turned in to applying for adoption. Immediately after his arrival in Minnesota, he was evaluated and subsequently diagnosed with a chromosomal syndrome, a diagnosis which answered many questions and determined the course of action moving forward. It had been responsible for many of his health issues including a damaged heart, which was immediately repaired by surgery. Three days after the surgery, he appeared at the courthouse in the county where Sara lived and was declared to be officially adopted by Sara and her husband. The journey had been one of frustration, perseverance, and faith. Sara states that when she weakened and felt she just couldn't go on any further with the process during those seven years, she kept trying to tell God no. She'd had enough. And always, he opened the next door that needed to be opened. It was a long journey, but Aaron had found his home. Sara never let go.

Today, Aaron is twenty-three years old and though he has many physical and cognitive limitations, he is living a life that would not have been possible if not for our church's decision to send teams to Sunbeam Children's Home to help make the lives of Jamaican children a little better.

In January 2003, I was provided a memorable experience at Kingston's Marigold Nursery. As we often did, we stopped here on our pilgrimage day to drop off a few donations and to spend some time with the children. This year, I was disappointed in the deterioration of the facility from my past visits. The babies just did not seem as well cared for this time around. None of the babies held out their arms to be picked up, even the few mobile ones, because they had not been conditioned to do so. With fifty-eight children in the home, the chances were simply non-existent that each child would get an adequate amount of individual touch and human contact.

Only the babies were visible to us, as the toddlers were in a back room attending their pre-school activities. Most of the babies appeared to have some sort of disability, some minor, some major. I made it a point to weave my way through the lined-up cribs, some of which contained more than one baby, and made eye contact and physically touched each child in some way. Some responded and some did not. Some smiled back when I smiled; most did not.

I made the decision to spend extra time with those who did not respond. I was curious if their lack of response was conditioned by neglect, or if they truly were not capable of responding. I focused for a while on a baby with deformed arms and legs, laying on her back in an awkward-looking position with a blank stare. Though she was the size of a baby, I think that she was perhaps a very underdeveloped and undernourished two- to four-year-old. When I smiled and spoke softly to her to try to get a response, it was if she was not there. So, I lowered my face right down into the crib in front of her face and smiled and made funny noises and bopped my finger on her nose and played peek-a-boo. I ran through what felt like my entire repertoire of baby entertainment. Sure enough, after a while a little smile, then a big smile came to this little girl's face. I could have cried. Maybe I did.

But pondering this little girl's smile afterward made me sad. Knowing she did indeed have the capability to respond and smile, I wonder how many times the staff members and perhaps other visitors had walked right past her crib and had not bothered to spend the time needed to give this little girl the pleasure of a smile, thinking she was unable to respond or worse yet, unworthy of their time, thinking their attention would not have made a difference.

I picked up her rather stiff, awkward body and cradled her for a while, and she maintained eye contact with me the whole time and gave me many more smiles. Her eyes were locked into mine. This little girl was equal in God's eyes to every privileged child in this world. I was frustrated that Jamaica seemed so determined not give up her children for adoption yet warehoused them in this way.

There were so many other skinny little kids like this little girl. They laid in their cribs with a variety of disfigured limbs, eyes that peered off in differing directions, crusty skin, runny noses, soaked and soiled diapers. Many had the rocking motion so prevalent in orphanages where human contact is inadequate. If only I could spend a day there, just holding babies. I couldn't do much for these kids, but that's something I could do. I would like to put my face right in their space and see if I could make every one of them smile at me. That would be a good day.

I knew I had to simply walk away. We placed the babies back in their cribs after holding and rocking them, and some cried. If there is a theme of my visits to the children's homes in Jamaica, it is that walking away is so hard. "Let it go, Heidi. Let it go," I would tell myself. "You can't fix this." One of the young men in our group was having an especially difficult time. He was a sensitive young man with a sweet and tender heart. It was hard to witness, but when I see reactions like this, I only briefly regret them, because I know this is God's way of speaking to us, of moving us.

Two years later, in 2005, we once again visited Marigold Nursery. That year it was so rewarding to travel with my daughter, Sara, as well as my friend, Cheryl. Cheryl and I went back into a small baby room that I had not realized existed when I had previously visited. The babies did at least have covered mattresses. Sometimes there are two babies in a small crib, but that was good as far as I was concerned. It provided a bit of comfort for each, as there were seemingly no toys, mobiles, or any sort of activity or stimulation for the babies.

Some of the babies were quite responsive, particularly a little guy named Glenroy who smiled and giggled at Cheryl and me the whole time. He was a chubby, healthy-looking little guy. But there were others who had the appearance of simply being warehoused there because of various disabilities.

I spent quite a bit of time holding a little guy, probably about six months old, who had Down Syndrome. When I asked the nurse what his name was, she said, "We're not sure; we call him Bert". It seemed so sad to me that this little boy did not have the dignity of having an official name. Bert was thin and not very responsive, and I could see from the reaction of the staff that he was not one that was held a lot or given much attention. It seemed clear to us, and so unfair, that there were favorites—the healthy, outgoing ones—and then a larger category of kids that got only the most basic attention. I focused my hugging on these.

Most of the other team could not bring themselves to spend much time in that baby room. It is understandable. It was my daughter Sara, Cheryl, and me. It was one of my most proud Mom moments in my daughter Sara's life up to that point. Rather than be repulsed or shy away from the very difficult environment we were in, she confidently walked into that back room with Cheryl and me and, following our lead, picked up babies and just seemed to know what to do. Her compassion took over. I remember thinking at the time, "She's going to be a great Mom someday," and she is. Most of our group stayed in the bigger room where the bigger babies or toddlers had their cribs, some stayed outside, and some could not bring themselves to get out of the bus. I understood.

In the nursery there were lots of misshapen little bodies; lots of self-stimulating behaviors due to lack of attention, affection, and stimulation: head banging and shaking, rocking, swaying back and forth, pulling hair. And lots of sad, blank, distant expressions. When our visit was done, it was extremely difficult to walk away. My own education had taught me that neglect has an immediate and long-term detrimental effect on the brain that literally affects how it is wired. Cognitive and emotional problems are almost certain in these kids. It was difficult to envision a bright future for them.

Many of us had a tough time putting down the kids because they screamed and cried and latched onto our legs. Pastor Corey took one for the team and stayed behind, grabbing the crying kids that we all had to put down, so that we could walk away. I had to pry a little boy out of her arms, then physically take Cheryl by the arm and lead her to the bus. I knew from the past that the only thing to do is walk away and not look back. It is the hardest thing you can imagine.

Letting go – the hardest lesson to learn.

During a visit to one of the other children's homes in 1995, at about two o'clock in the afternoon we handed out coloring books to all the kids who seemed able to handle one, and three large color crayons. Other children received a different kind of toy. The kids were thrilled with them, and many kids were still coloring as we left about five o'clock that day. It was admittedly frustrating to us to witness one of the helpers walk out the door that day with several coloring books tucked under her arm. We heard the same thing happened with light bulbs.

We could only justify this by rationalizing that their families probably needed them just as badly. We learned that the staff of some of these children's homes sometimes tended to hoard the items that they needed back in the day. These were not bad people. One comes to understand that stealing can be a means of survival in Jamaica. Things can be used in their own homes or traded or sold for food or other needed items. People try to take care of their families as best as they can, in whatever way they can. A difficult concept for newcomers to understand is that we cannot use our American frame of reference when judging behavior of people in a different culture. It is difficult, of course. But it served as another way to reinforce the important lesson that we must simply let go.

Alphonso was a boy that many of us got to know after the first few visits to Sunbeam. He had an engaging, endearing personality, a good heart, and a big mischievous smile. Full of creative talent, some of us called him "Sunbeam's artist." One day in late 1998 he got into a fight at Sunbeam and was dismissed from the home permanently by Mrs. Lue who, at the time, ran the home with Pastor Lue, and made such decisions regarding the boys. She had been particularly dismayed with the behavior of the older boys who, in those days, were allowed to stay well beyond their eighteenth birthday. Mrs. Lue had run out of patience with the older boys, and even though Alphonso was only seventeen, he was unfortunately the next one to act out, and was told to leave. He was sent home to his mother and grandmother, who lived in a small shack with one single bed. This living situation did not last long before his family sent Alphonso away. He soon ended up alone, like so many other young Jamaican children, trying to survive on the dangerous streets of Kingston.

In Chapter Nine, I wrote of our pilgrimage days and some of the activities we engaged in on that day. On this day in 1999, our pilgrimage took us to Kingston and then, to Port Royal. One does not travel into Kingston without a local Jamaican with knowledge of safe and unsafe areas to visit. Our trusty bus driver and tour guides, Ernest "Pooh" and Marla, were our keepers, guides, and protectors. We could not have done any of the off-site traveling we did without their guidance and protection. As American visitors, for example, we would not have known to avoid high-threat areas of Kingston such as Mountain View, Trench Town, Tivoli Gardens, Arnett Gardens, Cassava Piece, or many other dangerous areas. We have been told that typically, crime is Jamaican-upon-Jamaican and revolves around drugs, gangs, politics, poverty, or in many cases, revenge. A violent drug culture exists in Kingston. And national and local elections are often marred with violence and fraud. Most crimes committed on tourists have to do with property, such as theft; nonetheless, Kingston is a dangerous city, and a local Jamaican protector is a necessity.

Patsy, then the Director of Sunbeam, had seen Alphonso a few months earlier, and had mentioned to us that he was not looking particularly well at that time. Our team had decided early in the week that we would like to invite a few of the former Sunbeam boys to join us on our pilgrimage day, both to check up on them and to provide them with a fun day and a full belly. Someone contacted Alphonso, as well as Zatarrah, a former Sunbeam boy now living in Kingston, and invited them to join us. Zatarrah had been removed from Sunbeam for coming home from school late three days in a row because he played basketball after school. There were suspicions that he was spending time with a girl, he was made an example, and it resulted in Zatarrah being thrown out. Unlike with Alphonso, Zatarrah had a cousin that took him in and gave him a job in a shop of some sort. Also, unlike Alphonso, Zatarrah looked relatively healthy when we reunited with him, and was wearing a new pair of jeans, a sign that things were going relatively well. Both were delightful guests on "our day off."

We had arranged for Alphonso to meet us at the market, and it was so good to see our boy, though sad at the same time. He was very thin, much thinner than when he lived at Sunbeam. Under his undersized tee shirt, we could see his ribs stick out on the front side and his shoulder blades stick out in the back. He had dark circles under his sunken eyes. He wore a pair of worn baggy jeans and oversize flip flops. Alphonso still had the infectious smile we all remembered, and it warmed our hearts when he remembered several of us and called us by name. He stated matter-of-factly that he now lives on the streets of Kingston and begs for food, generally sleeping on the beach when and if he can find a safe spot. If not, he wanders through the night so that he can be more aware of his surroundings and tries to sleep during the daytime when it is safer.

We ended our pilgrimage day by eating a meal at a beautiful tourist hotel restaurant, sitting on a pier overlooking the ocean. Zatarrah stood up and gave a very touching thank you as we all sat at the table finishing our meal. He thanked us for bringing him and Alphonso along on our pilgrimage day, for the good meal in their bellies, and for the fellowship. He spoke sincerely of his time at Sunbeam, the love he had for his Sunbeam brothers, and for the positive influence teams like ours had had on his life. Zatarrah spoke articulately and authentically. I remember thinking at the time, "How dare we not be thankful for the things we Americans have, when a young man like Zatarrah, who grew up with so little, was so sincere and thankful for something as simple as a day of laughter and fellowship and a good meal?" Truly a perspective-changer for me.

After our meal, it was time to load up in the bus and get driven back to Sunbeam. We left Port Royal and were going through a dirty, noisy, crime-ridden part of downtown Kingston on a Saturday night, where Alphonso wanted to be dropped off. Our sweet Alphonso looked so small, and left us with a smile and a wave, belying the reality that he had no idea where he would sleep that night or where his next meal would come from. There was a noticeable silence on the bus after Alphonso stepped into the dark. Yes, we gave him some food to bring with him and some Jamaican cash, and we wished him Godspeed. But it was another instance in which we simply had to let him go and leave him in God's hands.

I do not recall receiving any update on Alphonso through the years. I think about him and how he, as a seventeen-year-old, endured the suffering he so obviously would have experienced on the streets. Alphonso is poverty and hopelessness with a name and a face and a personality.

It is always satisfying, yet sad. Every year, I feel sorry for the boys on our final evening, as they are so sad to see us go. We are told by the staff that on the days after our team leaves, the boys are much quieter, clearly sad. They will not get the attention they have enjoyed the last week. We leave these boys in God's hands, hoping they will reflect on our visit and look forward to our next one. Each boy processes our departure in his own way. Dwayne, age 13, who had been my special friend for the previous few years, and with whom I had gotten quite close, pushed a note into my hand as I walked out the door on the last day of our visit in 2003. It said, in his own spelling and word choice, *"Miss Hidy, You make me happy. I miss you when your gone. I will see you in heaven. Dwayne."* My heart cracked in two.

    I still have that note, written sixteen years ago, and it is a reminder of the hardest lesson: Sometimes we must let go and move on. We leave Sunbeam as different people than when we came. And we can only hope that we have left something with the boys that they did not have before we arrived. That is my wish every single time I leave Jamaica.

Chapter 14

Lesson: Trust God, But Bring Your Common Sense

On our 1997 visit, we arrived with a bit of time to kill before heading across the island to Sunbeam. Someone had the idea that we could perhaps find some good, live reggae music to get the true Jamaican music experience. So, while in the bus, we used Pooh and Marla's advice to find a Jamaican night club. But it didn't work out as we had planned. Even though we had our Jamaican friends with us, who normally serve as our bodyguards, we found that we were very much NOT welcome at the "Cactus," Spanishtown's biggest night club at the time.

Michael, our Jamaican guide, was told, as we all got off the bus, that he should "take his white friends and their money and leave." We apparently did not meet the dress code, as we were wearing tennis shoes and t-shirts. We left for our own safety. We spent some time driving around Spanishtown and enjoyed seeing the Saturday night life in the small Jamaican towns. The people really hit the streets on Friday and Saturday nights, but many years later, I am now appalled at the brazenness and frankly, our stupidity, for agreeing to try out the

"Cactus." After all, *"Cockroach neba so drunk him walk inna fowl yard"* (A cockroach is never so drunk that he would walk into a yard full of chickens) (McLean, 113). We always need to be responsible for our behavior, in every circumstance. As leader of the group, I had a lapse in judgment.

When we are at Sunbeam, we are very aware of the need for security, even inside the building. Throughout the week, we take turns hanging the keys for our dorms around our necks, and the others need to find the key-keeper to get in. In recent years, we admittedly have not been as vigilant about locking up, but we know it is not wise to relax in this area. It is important to lock up the dorms so that our personal possessions are safe, as well as all the tools and supplies we keep in there. At night, we are locked in, and have bars on all the windows, so it is critical to keep the key hanging right by the door so that we can get out in the event of a fire or other emergency.

One day in 2000, we learned the value of always having a Jamaican with us. Two of our seventeen-year-old team members rode with our Jamaican neighbor John to get some needed supplies for one of our work projects. As they were in a line-up of cars at a stop sign, a group of young Jamaican men wielding knives approached the car in a threatening way, seeing Americans. In rural Jamaica at that time, *Americans = money*. I am sure they intended to rob the boys but stopped when they saw neighbor John sitting in the back seat. Our guys were pretty shaken by the incident, and I used this event as an example that night in the team meeting of how important it is to stick together and to always have a Jamaican with us, preferably more than one.

In 2005, our pilgrimage day plans needed to be changed somewhat due to safety concerns. We eliminated a few of the stops we were originally going to make in inner city Kingston. Gang violence is rampant in Kingston, and one of the dons had been killed a few days prior to our visit there. This caused a great deal of unrest, gunfire, and violent crime. In addition, a white missionary was killed the day before we were to go there. Our bus driver, Pooh, told us that it would be very dangerous for us to be in that area, and that was the area in which the food kitchen, the AIDS baby home, and the nursing home we were planning to visit were located. So, we changed plans and visited facilities in other parts of town.

I like to control things in my own way. Like most people, I guess, I find it difficult for my competent self to give up control and understand that…gulp…God's way is better than my own. I seem to always need help to automatically seek him first and give him the wheel. Carrie Underwood, singing her "Jesus, Take the Wheel" should probably be piped into my home, my car, and every single place that I go… *"Jesus, take the wheel; Take it from my hands; 'Cause I can't do this on my own. I'm letting go, So give me one more chance, And save me from this road I'm on."* For the Christian, this is one of those bottom-line sorts of things. Like so many things, it's all about keeping a healthy balance: thinking logically, safely, and intelligently about things, but not stressing over it or trying to control those things. It's all about trust. And leading a group of people on a mission experience in a third world country is a good way to reinforce the need to both trust in God but pack the common sense.

Chapter 15

Lesson: It's Good to Go Home

I AM FORTUNATE that "going home" always had a positive connotation throughout my life. I was raised in a happy, stable home by two amazing parents, and sought to create that same dynamic when my husband and I established our own home and family. It is not lost on me that I have lived a life of privilege, not in terms of money and resources and possessions but in stability, satisfaction, and love. Oh, we all have our days. We have had challenges which, at the time, sometimes seemed unsurmountable. But I have lived a good life and home has been a good place to be. *It's good to go home.*

I initially intended to focus this discussion on the experience of going home to Minnesota after our visits to Sunbeam Children's Home. Sometimes one feels like it has been a month or a year rather than a week, and no one will argue that returning to a hot shower, a private bathroom, and in my case, a bottle of Diet Pepsi, is sweet after some time at Sunbeam. One returns with a fresh perspective on possessions, needs, and worldview, as well as the intense need to tell the stories.

But what has resulted instead is a lot of reflection on what *home* really means and, as a result, an expanded view of *going home*. I have learned that going home not only means, in my life, a return home to Minnesota, but also a return home to Sunbeam. Home is a place that provides a sense of belonging and identity. It is where you feel comfortable and welcome. You belong. You can be yourself. It is a place that comes without question and feels right. Your heart is there. While my Minnesota home and family will always have the firmest grip on my heart, I have realized that all the ways I describe the word *home* perfectly describe the way I feel as I walk into Sunbeam's front door and see the things that are so familiar to me. So, I do not just go home to Minnesota. I go home to Sunbeam.

Many of us from Peace Church have returned to Jamaica again and again, and there is little we love more than to ride up to Sunbeam's gate, step out of the bus, and walk in to a familiar, special place that truly feels like home. I will never get tired of seeing this painted on Sunbeam's living room wall, as it has been for the past 25 years: "How good and pleasant it is when brothers dwell together in unity" (Psalm 133). Even though we will most likely have been on some sort of transportation for perhaps eighteen hours or more at the time of our arrival at Sunbeam, the words of the old Danish proverb, *The road to the house of a friend is never long,* could not be more accurate. We are always greeted with smiles, hugs, and many excited boys, who have been hearing about our arrival for a long time and have been looking forward to it. "Miss Cindy!" "Miss Sherry!" "Miss Becky!" "Miss Heidi!" It is music to our ears.

The concept of home is not so clear for many of the Sunbeam boys. Many boys come to Sunbeam from homes where poverty, abuse, or other sad life circumstances blur the idyllic feeling of home that many of us have. Sunbeam provides a new, safe home for them; yet they miss their own home and family, because that home and family is the only home and family they ever knew. That sense of familiarity and belonging still pulls at their hearts. It used to be that there was little emphasis in re-homing the kids who resided in Jamaica's children's homes. It was very common for us to see the same boys for ten or more years, some spending their entire childhood at Sunbeam. With Jamaica becoming more and more westernized over the past twenty-five years, there has been an increased emphasis on keeping the children in the Children's Services facilities only until they are able to return to their own home and family. For some, this is realistic and serves as motivation for the child to meet behavior goals and other conditions. For others, it is a frightening prospect.

Regardless of each boy's situation, the important thing I have learned is that Sunbeam provides a safe, warm place for these boys to live as brothers for whatever amount of time they are there. One of the Sunbeam boys rode a city bus to school every day back and forth from Sunbeam. Every single day, twice per day, the bus took him past the home where he once lived with his mother and siblings. Every day he saw this home and could have made the choice to get off the bus and go back to that home. Instead, in the morning he stayed on the bus and continued to school. And after school, he stayed on the bus and continued home to Sunbeam. *Home* can be complicated.

A boy named Richard had no family involved in his life after his birth. He was given up as a baby and first lived at Glenhope Nursery, a place we have visited multiple times over the years I have traveled to Jamaica. He then lived at Strathmore Children's Home, another place I have referenced repeatedly in this book. The Peace Team was in Jamaica in 2004 when Richard arrived at Sunbeam as a five- or six-year-old. He was, and remains, a wonderful boy with a gentle soul. A local Jamaican church sponsored Richard, and when we visited in 2014, a woman from that church stopped by Sunbeam on Richard's birthday and presented him with a big birthday cake to share with his Sunbeam brothers, as well as two gifts: a wristwatch and some cologne. The church representative presented these things to Richard at our evening program, and it was such a pleasure to sing a robust "Happy Birthday" to him that evening. Richard is one boy that truly sees Sunbeam as home and the Sunbeam boys as his brothers.

During our 2003 trip to Sunbeam, I was getting acquainted with some of the little guys that were new since my previous visit. Junior and Jermaine, brothers, arrived sometime in the previous two years when I was not there. Junior was eleven years old, and Jermaine was ten. They had come to Sunbeam, as most of the boys did, through the court system, where they were processed by Jamaica Children's Services after being picked up from a Kingston ghetto.

Both were physically and verbally abused by their father, with whom they lived. Their mother had previously moved out of the home to live with another man. Junior and Jermaine were sent by their father to beg daily for money and food on the streets of Kingston. Both were deprived of any formal education until they arrived at Sunbeam. Junior seemed to me to be very intelligent. He loved school and he loved to study. He soaked up any opportunity to learn something new. It was sad to think of the time that had been lost in educating this guy. At eleven years of age, he could not read. Though a sweet boy and eager to learn, Junior was very aggressive, and got in fights frequently at Sunbeam. He told me he wanted to be a soldier when he grew up. His past life in an abusive home and his experiences on the streets of the Kingston ghetto had clearly scarred him, and it would take the grace of God to calm his soul. I have thought of him often, wondering if he managed to thrive despite his past life experiences.

Junior's younger brother, Jermaine, also could not read. Scarred, like his brother, from an abusive young life, Jermaine had a long way to go, but he seemed to have the gentle spirit that his older brother lacked. Jermaine was cooperative and polite most of the time, rarely got into fights with the other boys, and seemed very thankful for things that were done for him.

What a load these boys carried on their shoulders. We gave them lots of hugs, and showed them that there are people in the world that want nothing from them other than the assurance that they are safe and happy. In Sunbeam, they had a roof over their head, food in their bellies, a haven from their past abuse, and a houseful of brothers and people who loved and cared for them. This is what home is, and this is what they found at Sunbeam.

Sometimes, boys truly have nowhere else to go, and live at Sunbeam for many years. However, there are many who do have families but for various reasons, do not currently live with them. The boy may have behavioral issues, he may have gotten in trouble with the law, or he may simply have been put out onto the street by a parent due to overcrowding in the home. The reasons are as varied as the number of Sunbeam boys. In a recent visit to Sunbeam in 2017, a new boy came to Sunbeam when our team was there and it seemed, at least outwardly, to be a positive, compassionate way to welcome a new boy. He was introduced to the group by Superintendent Whitley during our evening program. Mr. Whitley spoke to the other boys as a group, telling the Sunbeam boys where their *brother* was from, where he would be sleeping, while affectionately holding his arm around the boy's shoulders. He encouraged the boys to welcome him and include him in their activities and reminded them that they were all brothers and that they needed to take care of each other. We all clapped and welcomed him, and gave our individual welcomes later, after the program. This boy had "come home," and though he was shy and at least somewhat apprehensive about this new living situation, he seemed to take it quite well and felt he was in a good place.

The situation could not have been more different twenty years earlier, back in 1997, when "coming home" felt completely different. I recall two new boys arriving the week the Peace team was there. The boys appeared to receive no official welcome, no hugs, no "orientation." They were shown their bed, and then basically let loose to find their way around the schedule and the social and physical structure of Sunbeam Children's Home. One of those children, Wayne, became the youngest Sunbeam boy upon his arrival at age seven. He was a small, shy boy who sucked his thumb. The story was that his family simply did not want him. So, he was physically abused and had had, by all accounts, a miserable life to that point. I knew that, given the circumstances in 1997, he would go through some sort of initiation by some of the other boys to show him the pecking order. They would intimidate him, hit him, and treat him badly.

Wayne looked so sad. He said he wanted a toy. And he said he would run away tomorrow. The other new boy, David, sat by himself that week and looked lonely. But David seemed to have more survival skills and I felt he would probably make it.

As it turned out, Wayne did not run away that week, and later in the week he appeared to be doing better. But I came to the sad and frightening realization that Wayne's gradual adjustment over the week had probably come due to the presence of our team, and soon we would be leaving. Many of us embraced him countless times when he had been crying, gave him special treatment, and tried our hardest to make him feel at home. I desperately pondered what he would do the next week when we all left. In praying about Wayne's situation, it came to me that Wayne's arrival may have been the purpose of our visit that week. If we accomplished nothing else, perhaps we prevented him from the desperation that he would have felt without us there and eased his transition from an abusive home to Sunbeam Children's Home.

"Coming home" does not always go smoothly, but Wayne eventually found his home at Sunbeam, as so many others did through the years and continue to do so today.

It's good to go home.

Epilogue

I sometimes wonder how long it will take for the tug of my heart toward Jamaica to ease. Maybe for the rest of my life, I will have two "homes," one of them being Sunbeam Children's Home. The circumstances of my life have changed. I am living a retired, snowbird life in which half of the year I am physically away from my church and physically removed from the planning and preparation phases of Jamaica missions. This makes it more difficult to have the same bonding experience with the team, thus making a mission team experience logistically more complicated.

Frankly, I cannot imagine *not* returning to this place that has captured my heart. But for now, I am content to simply reflect on my many years of Jamaica missions and my Jamaica boys, and the lessons they have taught me:

It's not the length of time, but the quality of the time that matters.

Sewing is a ministry. Laundry is a ministry. Anything can be a ministry.

Prepare, then leave the rest to God.
Be thankful for every sense.
Celebrate the ordinary.
Find joy.
Take care of yourself.
Be patient.
Take care of each other and allow others to take care of you.
People suffer in God's world.
We share the world with God's creatures.
Let go.
Trust God but bring your common sense.
It's good to go home.

WORKS CITED

Eisley, Loren. "The Star Thrower" in The Unexpected Universe. Boston, MA: Mariner Books, 1972 (originally published 1969)

Lawrence, Leota S. "The Historical Perspective of the Caribbean Woman." Negro Historical Bulletin 47.1-2 (1984): 37

McLean, Beresford. Jamaican Book of Proverbs. Maitland, FL: Mill City Press, 2018.

Morris, Mervyn, ed. Louise Bennett, Selected Poems. Kingston, Jamaica: Sangster, 1982. National Institute of Health. www.ncbi.nim.nih.gov/pubmed/28375542. Online. 21 Feb 2020

Rettner, Rachel. Brains Link Between Sounds, Smells and Memories Revealed. Online. www.livescience.com. 5 Aug. 2010.

Thompson, Thelma. "Their Pens, Their Swords: New Jamaican Women Poets and Political Statement in Nation Language." Studies in Literary Imagination 26.2 (1993): 45-63. www.britannica.com/place/Jamaica/economy. Online. 6 May 2020

CPSIA information can be obtained
at www.ICGtesting.com
Printed in the USA
BVHW072101291121
622782BV00010B/274